P9-DNK-938

RICHARD ROHR

WONDROUS ENCOUNTERS

SCRIPTURE

FOR

LENT

ST. ANTHONY MESSENGER PRESS
Cincinnati, Ohio

Cover and book design by Mark Sullivan
Cover image © istockphoto.com | Alf Ertsland

LIBRARY OF CONGRESS CATALOGING-IN-PUBLICATION DATA
Rohr, Richard.
Wondrous encounters for Lent / Richard Rohr.
p. cm.
ISBN 978-0-86716-987-4 (alk. paper)
1. Lent—Meditations. 2. Bible—Meditations. 3. Catholic Church—
Prayers and devotions. I. Title.
BX2170.L4R64 2011
242'.34—dc22

2010032449

ISBN 978-0-86716-987-4

Copyright ©2011, by Richard Rohr. All rights reserved.

Published by St. Anthony Messenger Press
28 W. Liberty St.
Cincinnati, OH 45202
www.AmericanCatholic.org
www.SAMPBooks.org

Printed in the United States of America.
Printed on recycled paper.

11 12 13 14 15   5 4

Contents

PREFACE

I wrote these Scriptural reflections during my lenten hermitage in Arizona in 2010. They came very easily and even quickly, which is the gift of long times of silence and solitude. I hope they will be a gift to you, especially to any of you who want to go deeper yourselves, or have been charged with the great work of preaching or teaching.

I suggested the title to the editors at St. Anthony Messenger Press because I was experiencing being caught up in a wondrous loop of realizations that kept tightening, revealing, and confirming themselves at ever deeper levels. There was the inner prayer that found itself in outer Scriptures, and written Scriptures that allowed me to trust and affirm my inner experience. There was a clear downward death cycle in the lenten readings which was inherently becoming an upward life cycle. It was a most contemplative time, and yet the social implications of the Scriptures were also undeniable from such a spacious place. Action and contemplation were in a clear embrace, needing and loving one another.

It was indeed wondrous for me how the synchronicities, signs, and symbols were soon appearing everywhere—in my study, in my prayer, in my long desert nature walks, and on the written page. The days were a constant flow. By the time I got to Holy Saturday, I realized that what

I would consider almost all of the major themes of Scripture, or at least Scripture as I understood it, had found their way onto paper! So I suggested that this not be presented as daily meditations, although I hope it would be that too, but a lenten-based encounter with the Bible itself. *Not just "what" is in the Bible, but more "how" we can interpret the Scriptures for ourselves, and grow through these parallel situations today.* Not so much information as an experience of transformation, not so much explanation as Encounter itself.

I thank dear Margaret Slattery for offering me her "hermitage" in well-named "Carefree" Arizona, so that I could be free to enjoy this time of immense grace and inner Sabbath, and write these reflections.

My hope and prayer is that the reading might be a real hermitage experience for you too, and your own kind of Encounter.

Richard Rohr
Lent 2010
Carefree, Arizona

The Wondrous Loop

There are two moments that matter. One is when you know that your one and only life is *absolutely valuable and alive*. The other is when you know your life, as presently lived, is *entirely pointless and empty*. You need both of them to keep you going in the right direction. Lent is about both. The first such moment gives you energy and joy by connecting you with your ultimate Source and Ground. The second gives you limits and boundaries, and a proper humility, so you keep seeking the Source and Ground and not just your small self.

The paradox, of course, is that you find yourself anyway: your Big Self in God and your little self in you. God loves them both. Saint Teresa of Avila summed it up when she said, "We find God in ourselves, and we find ourselves in God." With such a maxim, she did not likely need a therapist. Yet, I would add, that it is always much more like being found than actually finding anything! As Paul put it, "then I shall know as fully as I am known" (1 Corinthians 13:12).

So during these forty days of Lent, let's allow ourselves to be known! All the way through. Nothing to hide from, in ourselves, from ourselves, or from God. Allow yourself to be fully known, and you will know what you need to know. This is my desire in writing these meditations. It is in this wondrous loop of divine disclosure, our own now safe self-disclosure, and a healing mutual acceptance—that we grow "in wisdom, maturity, and grace" (Luke 2:40). In fact, that is the way that all love happens, and the only way we grow at all.

I will begin each meditation with a single title or phrase that for me sums up the point. One-liners can often be remembered more than paragraphs. Then I will reverse the common process, and offer you the meditation first—and then key passages from the readings afterward. I hope that will allow you to read the precise Scripture with clarity, insight—and new desire! I have found that in the spiritual life, less is always more. Long, or too many Scriptures, just keep us from needed focus and impact. We do not know where to look and so end up looking nowhere, and then leaving in a muddle of pious confusion. A little bit of God's Word goes a long way. To do this best, I will compose a legitimate Scripture translation from several sources, usually a combination of the *New American Bible*, the *Jerusalem Bible*, and sometimes with some inspiration from *The Message* translation of Eugene Peterson, which is often brilliant. You will not be disappointed or misled. If this leads you to check out the Scripture passage with your own translation, that is even better.

Since many Christians tend to read or recite prayers, instead of praying from the heart, I am deliberately not going to compose full prayers for you each day. I will offer you an invitation to your own self-disclosure to the Holy One—a "starter prayer," as it were. I want you to get inside this wondrous loop of divine dialogue for yourself, and in your own conscious and sincere words.

These meditations on the daily readings of Lent are not for the sake of mere information, or even for academia (although I hope it will satisfy both), but for the sake of our transformation into our original "image and likeness," which is, we are told, the very image of God (Genesis 1:26). What always and finally matters for all of us is *the Encounter itself!*

ASH WEDNESDAY
Another Start!
2 Corinthians 5:20—6:2

It seems that we need beginnings, or everything eventually devolves and declines into unnecessary and sad endings. You were made for so much more! So today you must pray for *the desire to desire!* Even if you do not feel it yet, ask for new and even unknown desires. For you will eventually get what you really desire! I promise you. It is the Holy Spirit doing the desiring at your deepest level. Therefore you will get nothing less than what you really desire, and almost surely much more.

You *are* the desiring of God. God desires through you and longs for Life and Love through you and in you. Allow it, speak it, and you will find your place in the universe of things. Now let me tell you something: You cannot begin to desire something if you have not already slightly tasted it. Now make that deep and hidden desire conscious, deliberate, and wholehearted. Make your desires good and far-reaching on this Ash Wednesday of new beginnings. You could not have such desires if God had not already desired them first—in you and for you and *as* you!

Remember finally, that the ashes on your forehead are created from the burnt palms of last Palm Sunday. New beginnings invariably come from old false things that are allowed to die.

Today's Readings

"We are ambassadors for Christ, God as it were appealing through us. We implore you in Christ's name: know that you are a friend of God!… We beg you not to receive this grace of God in vain. God has already said, 'In a favorable time I have heard you; on the day of salvation, I have helped you' [Isaiah 49:8]. Well, now is that favorable time! Today is the day of salvation!"

2 Corinthians 5:20; 6:1–2

Starter Prayer

"God, give me the desire to desire what you want me to desire."

THURSDAY AFTER ASH WEDNESDAY
Decision Precedes Depth
Deuteronomy 30:15–20; Luke 9:22–25

I once wrote a book on non-dual thinking. This is the way the saints and mystics think, not *either-or* but *both-and*. It is the inner hardware which makes them able to forgive, overlook offenses, show mercy to all, care for the poor, and even to love their enemies. Most of us know we should do these things, but frankly we do not know *how*.

As I began to teach on this subject, many rightly pointed out that the Bible seems to have a lot of dualistic thinking in it too. We will see this today in both Moses and Jesus who set before us clear and urgent choices. We have only one life, and great teachers know that we must discover our true destiny, which we call "saving our soul." At some point in life, this calls for some clear choices: "blessing or curse" in Moses' language, "true self and false self" in Jesus' terms.

Only people who first choose "dualistically" for the Big Picture, the life adventure, the journey with God, eventually proceed to non-dual thinking or "mercy." Sort of a paradox, isn't it? You need both to go the full distance. Clear choice and decision gets you started, aims you on the right course, and then if you stay on it, that very path will open you up to subtlety, nuance, shadow, contradictions, inconsistencies, brokenness, and variance in almost everything. One soon realizes that what Jesus said is indeed true: Nothing is entirely good except God alone (see Mark 10:18). The choice for this all-good God allows us, ironically, to deal victoriously with non-goodness.

So first we must place our bet, set our trajectory, make a choice, surrender to the Great Love. That is the initial dualistic call and clarification that we hear in all the Jewish prophets and in Jesus: God or Mammon, sheep or goats, the narrow gate, the sharp and painful sword of discernment and choice. But just be ready for the trials and confusion that this clear choice will lead you into. Yes, the field closed down, but it also opened up. The main difference is that now the issues are *real!*

Today's Readings

"I call heaven and earth to witness this. I now set before you life and death, a blessing and a curse. Choose life then, that you and your descendents will live, by loving the Lord, heeding the voice, and clinging to God."

Deuteronomy 30:19–20

"Whoever would save his life must first lose it, and whoever loses her life for my sake will find it. What profit does she show who gains the whole world yet destroys herself in the process?"

Luke 9:24–25

Starter Prayer

"Lord, show me how to make good decisions and then be willing to learn what they really ask of me."

FRIDAY AFTER ASH WEDNESDAY

Our Amazing Capacity for Missing the Point

Isaiah 58:1—9a; Matthew 9:14—15

Isaiah, purified after the great exile, defines fasting in a whole new and rather "secular" way. It is courageous that the church dares to use such a hard-hitting passage at the beginning of Lent, considering that the very same situation still applies today. Some scholars say that it was this kind of writing that got Isaiah killed. He accuses and condemns his fellow Jews for "afflicting themselves" and "bowing their heads" through ritual observances, fasting, and formal temple prayers, but largely missing the whole point of religion. This passage would not have been a big hit with the pious, the priestly class, or the temple conservatives of Isaiah's day.

Isaiah says explicitly that God prefers another kind of fasting which changes our actual lifestyle and not just punishes our body. (The poor body is always the available scapegoat to avoid touching our purse, our calendar, or our prejudices.) Isaiah makes a very upfront demand for social justice, non-aggression, taking our feet off the necks of the oppressed, sharing our bread with the hungry, clothing the naked, letting go of our sense of entitlement, malicious speech, and sheltering the homeless. He says very clearly this is the real fast God wants!

It is amazing that we could ever miss the point. It is likely that what we later called the corporal works of mercy came from this passage. We can presume that Jesus was familiar with it because of his parallel sermon on the sheep and the goats.

The passage segues nicely into the short gospel on why Jesus and his disciples do not fast. In effect, he says "because it is the wrong kind of fasting!" Then he introduces a favorite theme and metaphor that he gradually develops: life as a wedding banquet, with himself as the bridegroom and humanity as the bride. It will soon become clear that Jesus is not interested in an elite who do their rituals properly yet refuse to join in the wedding feast that God is preparing for *all*, both insiders and outsiders.

Today's Readings

"Cry out full-throated and unsparingly, lift up your voices like a trumpet blast! Tell the people their actual wickedness, let the people know their real sins.... 'Is this the kind of fasting I wish? Do you call this a fast day acceptable to God?'"

Isaiah 58:1, 5

"Why is it that while we and the Pharisees fast, your disciples do not?"

Matthew 9:14

Starter Prayer

"God, what is it that you want me to let go of this Lent? Is it other than what I think?"

SATURDAY AFTER ASH WEDNESDAY
A Double Punch
Isaiah 58:9b–14; Luke 5:27–32

I hate to tell you, but yesterday's hard-hitting passage from Isaiah continues today, although it does now turn toward the positive. Here Isaiah tries to describe what a just people and country would look like if they fasted from the right things. He uses lovely words like light, guidance, abundance, renewed strength, watered gardens, repairers and restorers, nurturance, and delight, "a spring that never fails," and even "riding on the heights of the earth." But it all depends on fasting from unkindness and choosing justice. It is this very passage speaking of "repair and restoration" (*tikkun*) that our Jewish brothers and sisters use today as their call to social justice.

The same refrain from yesterday also continues in Jesus. He is again accused of eating with the wrong people at the house of another wrong person, Levi the tax collector. Anybody who cooperated with the Roman oppressors was by definition and social position a "sinner." Jesus is "cooperating with evil" and "complicit" in their sin, a good patriot or churchgoer would say both then and now. Yet Jesus reminds them that their definition of "holiness as separation from" is entirely wrong (see Leviticus 11:24). Jesus has a different agenda and strategy, even though this wrong "law of holiness" continues in all immature religion to this day. Jesus has come to transform people, not to exclude them. He has come for the seeming losers, and not to create a country club for the supposed winners.

Today's Readings

"If you remove from your midst oppression, false accusation, and malicious speech, if you bestow your bread on the hungry, and satisfy the afflicted, *then* light shall rise for you in the darkness,…and God will guide you always, and give you relief in desert places."

Isaiah 58:9–11

"The healthy do not need a doctor, but sick people do. I have not come to coddle the comfortable, but to set trapped people free for a new life."

Luke 5:31–32

Starter Prayer

"God, where am I trapped and unable to see it?"

Temptations Are Attractions to Partial Goods

Mark 1:12—15; Matthew 4:1—11; Luke 4:1—13

In all three Lectionary cycles, the Gospel for the first Sunday of Lent is devoted to the temptation scene of Jesus in the desert from Matthew, Mark, or Luke. That seems to be the way that he experiences his forty days in the desert, so it seems like an appropriate way to start ours. This makes our chosen theme here rather clear, but as we examine it, it actually is not clear at all.

First, if Jesus is purely and simply "God," as many Christians seem to have concluded, then how or why can God be tempted? In fact, the texts appear to make Satan stronger than Jesus in some ways. We clearly have a very different image of both Jesus and God today than Matthew, Mark, or Luke do. (The theology of the "Hypostatic Union" has not yet emerged to try to describe this paradox.)

Second, even if Jesus were merely a human, then what precisely is the meaning of these temptations to his humanity? That would seem to be the meaning and application for us today. In short, I see the three temptations as the primal and universal temptations that all humans must face before they dare take on any kind of power—as Jesus is about to do. They are all temptations to the misuse of power for purposes less than God's purpose. They are sequentially the misuse of practical everyday power, the misuse of religious power, and the misuse of political power. These are the constant tragedies that keep defeating humanity. Jesus passes all three tests, and thus "the devil left him" because he could not be used for lesser purposes. If you face such demons in yourself, God can and will use you mightily. Otherwise, you will, for sure, be used!

But let me point out something we almost always fail to notice. We can only be tempted to something that is good on some level, partially good, or good for some, or just good for us and not for others. Temptations are always about "good" things, or we could not be tempted: in these cases "bread," "Scripture," and "kingdoms in their magnificence." Most people's daily ethical choices are not between total good and total evil, but between various shades of good, a partial good that is wrongly perceived as an absolute good (because of the self as the central reference point), or even evil that disguises itself as good. These are what get us into trouble.

Jesus is the master of spiritual discernment here, which is always much more subtle and particular than mere obedience to external laws. Note that Jesus quotes no moral commandments here, but only wisdom texts from Deuteronomy.

Today's Reading

"The Spirit drove Jesus into the wilderness, where he stayed for forty days. There he was put to the test by Satan. He was with the wild beasts, yet angels ministered to him."

Mark 1:12–13

Starter Prayer

"God, help me to distinguish my wild beasts from my angels. Help me to see how I often confuse one with the other."

The Important "Commandments" Are Not Always Seen

Leviticus 19:1–2, 11–18; Matthew 25:31–46

If you read the First Reading from today's Lectionary, you will note that it is from the Hebrew book of Leviticus 19 and sounds a bit like the more common version of the Ten Commandments that we all grew up with that is found in Exodus 20, yet is also very different. In both places there is a lot of verbiage before, during, and after, which makes the precise "ten" commandments not so clear or apparent, and makes one wonder how God got it all written on those tablets of stone that Moses was able to carry down the mountaintop. Maybe Moses had a donkey or a dolly. No wonder he broke them!

The important Gospel today is from Matthew 25, which is his final judgment scene. It seems to be placed in perfect juxtaposition to the Hebrew Ten Commandments. They are like two bookends revealing the beginning and conclusion of the great Judeo-Christian tradition, and even the tasks of the two halves of life.

Leviticus begins with the clear goals and boundaries that are necessary for the sake of a moral and a religious society, and the tangent is set in motion with the final so-called "Golden Rule." This all leads and develops to create the Jesus phenomenon, and what could well be called Jesus' "commandments," which go far beyond mere boundary-keeping to actually moving beyond all boundaries to take care of those who did not make it, do not fit in, the outsider, the criminal, the vulnerable, and the weak. It is quite a leap which, to be honest, many Christians have never made. You could obey the Ten Commandments perfectly all of your life and never come close to the mark that Jesus sets for the final judgment. Yet the promise and seed is entirely there in Leviticus 19:18: "You must love your neighbor as you love yourself."

The final leap that Jesus makes is even more astounding. He not only creates a moral equivalence between me and my neighbor, but finally between my neighbor and God! "What we do to others, even the least of the others, we do to God," he says! It is almost too much to comprehend and surely leaves all of us among the goats.

Today's Readings

"Be holy (whole) as I your God am holy (whole)…. Show neither partiality to the weak, nor deference to the mighty, but judge all justly."

Leviticus 19:2, 15

"I assure you, whatever you did for one of the least of these, you did for me.... Whatever you neglected to do for one of the least of these, you neglected to do for me."

Matthew 25:40, 45

Starter Prayer
"Loving God, allow me to be a sheep at least once in a while, and never let me forget that most of my life I have been a goat."

TUESDAY OF THE FIRST WEEK OF LENT
Certain Eventual Results
Isaiah 55:10–11; Matthew 6:7–15

I must tell you that the First Reading today, which is the short but lovely conclusion of Second Isaiah's "Book of Consolation," is one of my favorites. It is poetic, intriguing, daring, and yet authoritative all at the same time. It is the reason I love the Jewish Scriptures and that Jesus was a Jew. This is the mind and heart that created him!

Here we have a writer in the fullness of the Babylonian exile, Jerusalem has fallen, no end in sight, and still he (some say "she"!) can speak with totally calm inevitability, kind certainty, and even joyful trust. (Treat yourself and open your Bible to 55:12–13 to see his or her final exclamation point, which is not included in the Lectionary reading.) While Isaiah is herself suffering, s/he still loves enough to want to make God "famous" and "ineffaceable"!

Then we have Matthew's version of the "Our Father," preceded by a warning against "rattling on" with too many prayers, and ending with a promise of a perfect and fair equivalence between how you forgive and how you will be forgiven. I mean no offense to our Catholic practice of confessing sins to a priest in order to be forgiven, but we must be honest and admit that Jesus made the essential requirement for the forgiveness of sin rather clear and definitive here: *As you do it, it will be done to you. If you do not do it, it cannot be done to you.*

We are merely and forever inside of the divine flow, just like Isaiah's "rain and snow." Forgiveness is not some churchy technique or formula. Forgiveness is constant from God's side, which should become a calm, joyous certainty on our side. Mercy received will be mercy passed on, and "will not return to me empty, until it has succeeded in what it was sent to do."

Today's Readings

"As the rain and snow come down from the heavens and do not return without watering the earth and making it yield… so the word does not return to me empty, without carrying out my will and succeeding in what it was sent to do."

Isaiah 55:10—11

"Forgive us our debts as we forgive others…. If you forgive the faults of others, your heavenly Father will forgive you yours. If you do not forgive others, neither can your heavenly father forgive you yours."

Matthew 6:12, 14—15

Starter Prayer

"Good God, keep me forever inside of your abundant and generous flow of mercy, toward me, through me, in me, and from me."

WEDNESDAY OF THE FIRST WEEK OF LENT

"No Sign Will Be Given Except the Sign of Jonah"

Jonah 3:1–10; Luke 11:29–32

Considering how Catholics love apparitions and miracles, how Protestants have made faith into a technique and formula, and how Evangelicals love a "totem and taboo" use of Scripture, this strong one-liner of Jesus feels rather amazing and largely unheard. He even says it is "an evil age" that wants anything other than the simple sign of Jonah. He says it is the "only sign" that he will give.

This is indeed unsatisfying. For it is not a sign at all, but more an anti-sign. It demands that we release ourselves into the belly of darkness before we can know what is essential. It insists that the spiritual journey is more like giving up control than taking control. It might even be saying that others will often throw us overboard, and that we get to the right shore by God's grace more than right action on our part. It is clearly a very disturbing and unsatisfying sign. And this is all we are going to get?

You see, faith is precisely no-thing. It is nothing you can prove to be right, or use to get anywhere else. If you want something to believe in (which is where we all must start!), you had best be a totem and taboo Christian, with clear ground, identity, and boundaries. But that is not yet faith! That is merely securing the foundations for your personal diving board.

Faith is the leap into the water, now with the lived experience that there is *One who can and will catch you*—and lead you where you need to go! Religion, in some sense, is a necessary first half of life phenomenon. Faith is much more possible in the second half of life, not necessarily chronologically but always spiritually. As the Danish philosopher Søren Kierkegaard wisely said, "Life must be lived forward, but it can only be understood backward." Jonah knew what God was doing, and how God does it, and how right God is—only *after* emerging from the belly of the whale. He has no message whatsoever to give until he has first endured the journey, the darkness, the spitting up on the right shore—all in spite of his best efforts to avoid these very things. Jonah indeed is our Judeo-Christian symbol of transformation. Jesus had found the Jonah story inspiring, no doubt, because it described almost perfectly what was happening to him!

Today's Readings
"The word of God came to Jonah: 'Set out for the great city of Nineveh, and announce to it the message that I will tell you.'"

Jonah 3:1

"This is an evil age. It seeks a sign. But no sign will be given it except the sign of Jonah."

Luke 11:29

Starter Prayer
"God of surprising journeys, help me to live my life forward, trusting that you are steering the ship. Help me to understand my life backward by seeing and forgiving the many 'signs of Jonah.'"

THURSDAY OF THE FIRST WEEK OF LENT
Taking One's Life in One's Hands
Esther C:12, 14—16, 23—25; Matthew 7:7—12

Although we would now have more than a bit of trouble with Queen Esther's nationalism, prayer for hatred, and desire for vengeance, we still place this part of her long prayer into the lenten Lectionary for some other good reasons. It is an excellent example of how the biblical text itself reveals both a movement forward into a gradual discovery of God and a simultaneous movement backward into a self-centered using of God for our own purposes. Both are often in the same text.

Jesus then makes clear in the Gospel that when we ask for things from God, it first says something about God (God is trustworthy, God is listening, God cares), but it also says something about our present state and ourselves. How can we hear both?

Did you know that you only ask for what you have already begun to experience? Otherwise it would never occur to you to ask for it. Further, God seems to plant within us the desire to pray for what God already wants to give us, and even better, God has already begun to give it to us! We are always just seconding the motion, but the first motion is always and forever from God. The fact that you prayed at all means God just started giving to you a second ago. Isn't that wonderful to know! He makes a further point that if we, "with all of our sinfulness," would not fail to respond to another, then how much more God.

God is always much better than the most loving person you can imagine, Jesus is saying. It is not that we pray and God answers. It is that our praying is already God answering within us and through us.

The only trouble with Queen Esther is that like so many people she made the first motion (which reflected her own small agenda), when true prayer is always *seconding the motion*—which motion always comes from God. Now hear the old Scripture anew, knowing you will now pray for what God already wants to give you and prompts within you, and that is why it will always happen (admittedly, often in a very different way than we first imagined!). But that is our final and full act of trust in a God who always gives us "good things"!

Today's Readings
"Ask, and you will receive. Seek, and you will find. Knock, and it will be opened to you.... If you, with all your sinfulness, know how to give good things to your children, then how much more will God give good things to those who ask."

Matthew 7:7, 11

"Treat others as you would have them treat you: this sums up all the law and the prophets as well."

Matthew 7:12

Starter Prayer

"God, if you ask us to treat others as we would have them treat ourselves, then help me to believe that you operate in just the same way. You must treat me exactly as I would want to be treated—at my truest and best level."

FRIDAY OF THE FIRST WEEK OF LENT
Rewards and Punishments Are Inherent

Ezekiel 18:21—28; Matthew 5:20—26

Often Christians dismissed the Eastern notion of *karma* as something pagan, fatalistic, or unbiblical. Actually, we said the same thing, but just in different ways, and both of today's readings are good examples of our different ways. The rather universal notion of karma is simply saying that "what goes around comes around." Nothing just goes away in the world of spirit, but reaps its own good fruit, or eventually bears the seed of its own destruction. Just wait long enough, and it is always true.

The prophet Ezekiel is making just such an advance in sixth-century-BC Jewish thinking here. He moves the whole notion of rewards and punishments to the now and to the individual level. Up to this point, human consciousness largely thought in terms of collective retribution or victory. The individual did not matter that much. So this is a major move forward in our understanding of the importance of each human soul—now. Ezekiel is saying loudly and strongly that your human life matters, your personal decisions and choices do define you. You have worth. Both individually and now! This gives a necessary significance, dignity, and urgency to the whole human journey.

Then Jesus, surely familiar with Ezekiel, spells out the same notion of inherent reward and punishment for his own contemporaries. Yet he goes even one step further and now localizes the core problem *inside* of the human person! Human consciousness is ready to be invited by him beyond mere external observance of rights and wrongs to inner attitudes, motivations, judgments, and opinions. If those are wrong or negative now, you are already in "Gehenna" (the perpetually burning garbage dump outside the Dung Gate of Jerusalem), and if you can "exceed the holiness of the scribes and Pharisees," you will be in "the kingdom of God"—now—and also later. We must not hear such readings as these as either a threat or a prize but rather as an invitation to human consciousness and the dignity of free will.

Today's Readings

"If a wicked person turns away from their evil and does what is right and just, they will surely live, they shall not die. None of the crimes they committed will be held against them."

Ezekiel 18:21

"You have heard the commandment imposed on your forefathers, 'You shall not commit murder, and every murderer shall be liable to judgment.' What I say to you is: everyone who even grows angry with his brother or sister shall be liable to judgment…and whoever holds him or her in that contempt, risks the fires of Gehenna."

Matthew 5:21–22

Starter Prayer

"Creator God, could it be true that you give me my human dignity and significance by asking so much of me? Do you respect me so much to hope that I could actually be like you?"

SATURDAY OF THE FIRST WEEK OF LENT

Commandment as a Big Push Over the Top

Deuteronomy 26:16–19; Matthew 5:43–48

I am afraid we are all born rather egocentric. We are the only reference point that we have, at least initially. "It's all about me, and why shouldn't it be?" If Mom and Dad mirror us well, we soon develop "mirror neurons" for empathy and relationship with others, but even other people can still be seen as mere means to my own power and pleasure. Or I can think I deserve everything, which we call a sense of entitlement. We all know adults who never seem to have moved beyond using other people and even using God; they seem to have an arrested spiritual and moral development. They seem unable to receive any true mirroring from God, nor do they lovingly mirror anyone else. They are trapped inside themselves.

Both readings today speak strongly of commandments, and even commandments that push us beyond our normal comfort zones. Moses admits that this will create a "peculiar" people "raised above all the other nations, a people sacred to God." Unless there is some pressure, social or parental, pushing the infant beyond the pleasure principle, human nature tends to largely take the path of least resistance. We really do need prods, goads, ideals to help us think outside of the little boxes we all create for ourselves. That is the function of laws and commandments. Only in the more mature person can love and grace take over—or even be understood.

Jesus builds on this basic impulse control to command, yes, command, the most difficult position of all: Love of the enemy! Prayer for the persecutor! He points out that this commandment is impossible with ordinary human motivation, or a philosophy of being nice to those who are nice to you. Anybody can do that, he says. Jesus knows he is moving the bar to a much higher plane, and it will be a necessary push to get us there: You are to love with the same kind of love that God loves you, which is total unconditional love. This is the summit and goal of all Jesus' moral teaching, and we cannot possibly follow it apart from divine union. The egocentric or separate self is incapable of this kind of love.

Today's Readings

"This day God commands you to observe these statutes and decrees with all your heart and with all your soul. . . . Yahweh is to be your God and you are to walk in God's ways and observe these commandments. You are to be a people peculiarly God's own."

Deuteronomy 26:16, 18

"This will prove that you are sons and daughters of your heavenly Father, for his sun rises on the bad and the good, he rains on the just and the unjust alike.... Live generously and graciously toward others, the way God does toward you."

Matthew 5:45–48

Starter Prayer

"God, I have to be honest with you. I am not sure I know how to do this. I am not sure I want to be one of your 'peculiar' people."

SECOND SUNDAY OF LENT
The Third Something
Luke 9:28–36

Since all three cycles of the Lectionary make "The Transfiguration" scene the Gospel for this Sunday, let's try to talk about it here—although surely in vain, since this is one of those passages that refuses to be "talked about," as Jesus himself commands when they descend from their mountaintop experience.

It is surely an archetypal and mystical account. The details are all in place. Taking ordinary people "up a mountaintop by themselves," sleepy men are about to be awakened. The stage is fully set for encounter and for divine intimacy. The "apparition" includes the two symbolic figures of Judaism—the law and the prophets—and the two halves of life—Moses and Elijah. Then Jesus appears between them "in dazzling white" that is always the inclusion of everything, all colors, as it were.

In seeing the reconciling third one, Jesus, the other two disappear. He synthesizes and moves beyond all dualisms. After this awesome and consoling epiphany, there is clear mention of "a cloud that overshadows" everything. We have what appears to be full light, yet there is still darkness. Knowing, yet not knowing. Getting it, and yet not getting it at all. Isn't that the very character of all true Mystery and every in-depth encounter?

The verbal messages are only two: "Beloved Sonship" and "Don't talk about it." Clearly Peter, James, and John experienced Jesus' beloved sonship, but also their own—in being chosen for such a mountaintop moment. Peter's response is the response of everyman and everywoman, "How good it is to be here!" yet it also expresses an emotion that is described as being "overcome with fear or awe"—exactly what Lutheran theologian Rudolf Otto called the *"mysterium tremendum,"* wondrous fascination and attraction together with a stunning sense of one's own littleness and incapacity, both at the same time! That is what holy moments always feel like: I am great beyond belief and I am a little dot in the universe.

This experience only needs to happen once, just as it did for Peter, James, and John. That is enough. It will change everything. It is available to all, and I believe, offered to all, at one time or another. You cannot program it, but you can ask for it and should expect it. You will never be able to talk about it, nor do you need to. Your ordinary shining life, different now down in the valley, will be its only and best proof.

Today's Reading

"Peter, and those with him, had fallen into a deep sleep, but on being awakened, they saw his glory.... And Peter said to Jesus, 'Master, how good it is to be here. Let me build three tents here, one for you, one for Moses, and one for Elijah.' He really did not know what he was saying.

And while he was speaking, a cloud came and overshadowed them all."

Luke 9:32–34

Starter Prayer

"Jesus, are such experiences just about you or are they also about us? Do you want us to think higher of you, or higher of ourselves because of you? Why do you take us along on such journeys at all?"

MONDAY OF THE SECOND WEEK OF LENT
Good Mirroring and Bad Mirroring
Daniel 9:4–10; Luke 6:36–38

It appears that humans can only know themselves through the gaze of others. We call it mirroring. A good parent, like God, naturally blesses the child through their receptive and affirming face. It is the eternal blessing to the children of Israel, "May Yahweh let his face shine upon you and be gracious to you. May Yahweh uncover her face to you and bring you peace!" (Numbers 6:25). Bad parents, that is to say, *not* like God, hand on their own self-rejection to their children.

In the First Reading from the book of Daniel, we see someone who is not being mirrored very well at all. The whole prayer appears to be guilt-based, fear-filled, self-hating, and self-rejecting. We are "shame-faced," Daniel says twice, and he projects his sad eyes onto "all the people of the land" who now share in his apparent unworthiness.

But thank God for the Gospel! Here we have total positive mirroring perfectly described. Receive God's compassion, and you will be able to be compassionate. Do not receive negative judgment from God, and you will not be judgmental yourself. Do not condemn and you will not be condemned. Give and it shall be given to you. Jesus describes a perfect reciprocity between what we have received or not received and how we will give or not give. It is all a matter of staying inside "the wondrous loop." Once you know that you are inside Trinitarian Love, you are connected to an infinite Source, and one is never sure who is doing the giving and who is doing the receiving. It is all Flow and Outpouring. It is you and yet it is God. Thus Jesus ends this Gospel by a wonderful image of overflowing abundance.

Today's Reading
"Full measure, pressed down, shaken together, running over, will be poured into your lap, because the measure you measure out with will be measured back to you."

Luke 6:38

Starter Prayer
"Mirror me like a magnet, good God. Don't let me be drawn into false, unhappy, or accusing faces. You are always and forever the Good Parent, and I long to see your face" (Psalm 42:2).

TUESDAY OF THE SECOND WEEK OF LENT
For the Sake of Change, Not Punishment
Isaiah 1:10, 16–20; Matthew 23:1–12

These are two hard readings today. The first is from the opening oracle of Isaiah, where he calls the religious establishment in Jerusalem "Sodom and Gomorrah," and commands them to seek social justice instead of their own advancement. Yet it is not merely to condemn them but to bring them to a new attitude, "Come let us set things right between us. Though your sins be like scarlet (and they are!), I want to make you white as snow," says Yahweh. How consoling and inviting God is, right after pulling no punches.

Then we see the same pattern in Matthew's Gospel. This is from Jesus' diatribe against the religious leadership of his time. Nothing any of us could say today would match Jesus' anger and judgment on hypocrisy in spiritual leadership and self-serving religious authority. He gets downright nasty with the leaders and mocks their religious fashion show and their unwillingness to "lift a finger to bear the burdens" that they place on other people. He seems to be against all titles that make them think they are higher or better than others, all lessons we could still learn today. I guess things never change.

Yet he ends by calling them to "humility" and promising them that God will do the "exalting." They do not need to worry about any climbing, self-promoting, or career advancement themselves.

Today's Readings

"Search for justice, help the oppressed, hear the orphan's plea, and defend the widow.... Though your sins be crimson red, I will make you white as wool, and you will eat the good things of the land."

Isaiah 1:17–18

"Their words are bold, but their deeds are few. They bind up heavy loads, hard to carry, to lay on other peoples' shoulders, while they themselves will not lift a finger to budge them.... You are all learners ["brothers"].... The greatest among you will be the one who serves the rest."

Matthew 23:3–4, 8, 11

Starter Prayer

"Humble God, make us like you. You do not lord it over us, but wait patiently for us to change. May we do the same with our brothers and sisters on the journey."

WEDNESDAY OF THE SECOND WEEK OF LENT
The Most Common Substitute for the Legitimate Suffering of the Self Is the Illegitimate Suffering of Others
Jeremiah 18:18–20; Matthew 20:17–28

If there is a constantly recurring theme in mythology, literature, and theater, it is that human beings who try to avoid changing themselves (an invitation which normally comes through "humiliating self-knowledge") always set out on a destructive course of trying to change the world, others, or even God. It is the old theme of *hubris* in Greek theater, and seems to be at the heart of every tragedy.

In its most dramatic form, of course, it even insists on the death of others and becomes murder, catastrophe, or war. Anything rather than change ourselves! Swiss psychologist C.G. Jung said that to avoid the "legitimate suffering" of being human, we inflict untold suffering on others, and finally actually bring more suffering on ourselves anyway. I find that to be profoundly true.

We see these patterns in both of today's readings. In the first from the prophet Jeremiah, we see "the men of Judah and the citizens of Jerusalem" plotting against his life. His truth-speaking has exposed their corruption, and he must be done away with. The part of the passage included seems to show that Jeremiah is forgiving, but if we read the whole prayer, we see that even he is eventually drawn into their cycle of vengeance and death.

Then in the Gospel, we see Jesus inviting his inner circle to follow him on the path of redemptive suffering instead of redemptive violence (which has been the accepted story line of almost all of human history). Jesus, against all odds, expectations, and human programming, insists that we make the preemptive and positive move into "drinking of the cup" ourselves instead of always asking others to drink it.

Note that two of the apostles send their mother to plead their case for *not dying*, but instead they want to be "enthroned"! The other ten are just jealous because they want the same. The whole scene is meant to be a laughable cartoon, and I am afraid it is a rather clear judgment on much of what became of the church, even in its leadership. I do not want to be unfair, but read our history—ecclesial and political. We still do not want to change ourselves; we want to change others instead.

Today's Reading

"From the cup I drink of, you shall indeed also drink.... Among the Gentiles, those who have authority lord it over others and make their importance felt. It must not be like that with you! Anyone who aspires to greatness among you must serve the rest, and anyone who wants to rank first among you, must serve the needs of all."

Matthew 20:23, 25–27

Starter Prayer

"Well, God, I sure do not like to hear this, but show me how it might be true in my life. Do I also 'kill' others as a substitute for those necessary deaths to myself?"

THURSDAY OF THE SECOND WEEK OF LENT

If You Don't Get It Now, You Won't Get It Then

Jeremiah 17:5–10; Luke 16:19–31

I must admit that I do not find any clear connection between the two readings for this day, and I do not especially like the first one. (There, I hope that gives some of you permission not to like some Scriptures. Frankly, I think many of them are regressive and small-minded.) This one is far too dualistic about the difference between trusting humans and trusting God. For the most part, I think we probably do both trusts about the same way. *How you do anything is how you do everything.*

But let's look at this intriguing Gospel, which is clearly a piece of Hebrew folklore that made its way into Luke's account and nowhere else. It has all the earmarks of old-time storytelling: a nameless rich man and a poor man with a beloved name like Lazarus, with dogs licking at his sores, "the bosom of Abraham" for heaven, and the pagan "Hades" for hell, then Abraham shouting answers across "the huge abyss that no one can cross."

This is a classic "reversal theme" which is so common in world literature and Scripture. The main sin of the rich man seems to be that he does not even notice the problem or the other man. He is blind and unaware of the pain of the world, while he eats "magnificently every day."

And the response of Abraham to him is this: "If you did not get it on that side of the abyss of life and death, why would you get it on this side?" There is presented a clear continuity between this world and the next. Or as some of our saints have said, "No one is going to be surprised in eternity!" We will all receive exactly what our lives say we really want and desire: Love is always torment for the hateful, and final torment is impossible for the loving.

Today's Reading

"If someone would go to them from the dead and tell them about this place of torment, they would repent,' said the rich man. 'No,' said Abraham, 'if they have not listened to Moses and the prophets, they will not be convinced by any voice from the dead either.'"

Luke 16:30–31

Starter Prayer

"God of life and death, help me to choose life now, help me to recognize love now, help me to see the poor in our world who long to eat the scraps that fall from our tables."

FRIDAY OF THE SECOND WEEK OF LENT

Don't Be Too Afraid of Being Thrown Into the Pit!

Genesis 37:3—4, 12—13, 17—28; Matthew 21:33—43, 45—46

I know that any kind of defeat or humiliation is not the American way, but it is surely the biblical way. There the pattern is rather clear, and there is no going up until you go down. Only our strong cultural bias, or a culpable blindness, would allow us to miss this central biblical theme that is everywhere in plain sight. The examples in Scripture are almost too numerous to count, ending of course, with Jesus himself in his Crucifixion and Resurrection.

In the First Reading we have the early part of the lovely Joseph saga, where in classic sibling rivalry and jealousy, Joseph's brothers throw him into the cistern, and then sell him into slavery to assuage any guilt over actually killing him. As always, some "manufactured difference" is used to justify the crime, so they write him off as a "master of dreams"! Little do they know that it will be this very dreaming that will one day free them.

Then we have the somewhat contrived allegory, sometimes called "the greedy farmhands." It is entirely characterized by what I would call a rejecting spirit. The farmhands just need to be antagonistic and oppositional about everything. They "beat, stone, and kill" everyone, and in the final verses Jesus seems to be aiming this parable at the religious authorities. Oppositional energy never knows what it is for, it just knows what it is against. It is sort of a sad substitute for vision, yet negative people feed on it.

This "spirit of rejection" is what kills Jesus, according to the quote that is pulled in from Psalm 118 at the end of the passage. Let's quote it in full here, because Jesus makes much of it, and realize that it equally applies to Joseph in the Hebrew Scriptures:

Today's Reading

"Did you never read in the Scriptures, 'The stone which the builders reject is in fact the cornerstone of the whole structure! It is the Lord who does it this way, and it is marvelous to behold.' It is for this reason that the kingdom of God will be taken away from you and given to others."

Matthew 21:42–43

Starter Prayer

"Patient God, is it really possible that so many of us could be that wrong? Why do we prefer the winners to the losers, when you were clearly one of the 'losers' and always on the side of the 'losers'?"

SATURDAY OF THE SECOND WEEK OF LENT
As Good as It Gets!
Micah 7:14–15, 18–20; Luke 15:1–3, 11–32

It is passages like this one from the prophet Micah that reveal how much Jesus was a Jew, knew the Hebrew Scriptures, and was deeply formed by them. If we do not fully appreciate this fact, then we try to know the *human text* (Jesus) outside of the clear and total *context* (post-exilic Judaism). Then the message is neither clear nor compelling.

How dramatic and alluring is Micah's statement that "God, who delights in clemency, and will again have compassion on us, will tread underfoot all of our guilt, and will cast into the depths of the sea all of our sins." What kind of experience of God allowed a peasant prophet to say such things on his own authority and eight centuries before Jesus said much the same? You have got to know this is quite amazing and game-changing.

Which leads to the *pièce de résistance* of all of Jesus' teaching, today's Gospel: the story that is strangely called "The Prodigal Son," even though it is much more about "The Prodigious Father" who is seemingly loving to excess! All scholars seem to agree that this story most perfectly represents Jesus' active and operative image of his personal experience of God. Frankly, if this is true, it changes everything, so let's quote the central passages here:

Today's Reading

"While he was still a long way off, his father caught sight of him, threw his arms around his neck, and kissed him.... 'Quick, bring out the finest robe and put it on him, put a ring on his finger and shoes on this feet. Take the fatted calf and kill it. Let us eat and celebrate because this son of mine was dead and has come back to life. He was lost and is found.' And the celebration began!"

Luke 15:20–24

Starter Prayer

"Well, good God, if this is true, I have had it all wrong up to now! Who are you? And who am I?"

THIRD SUNDAY OF LENT
If We But Knew the Gift of God!
John 4:5–42

This long and truly mystical Gospel story of the Samaritan woman at the well was already used by the early church in immediate preparation of the new candidates for baptism on Holy Saturday. All the elements of invitation, disclosure, unfolding levels of meaning, intimacy, reciprocity, and enlightenment are here for the taking. This multileveled story surely deserves our overall theme of a "wondrous encounter" of giver, given, and gift.

As is often the case, the story is also a reversal theme (who is giving to whom?), a first-level misunderstanding, an ethical bump in the road, and a deeper conversation, all to move the sincere reader to a needed seeking and questioning, which is exactly what we should want in all Christian beginners. This text could actually be used to exemplify a non-fundamentalist approach to Scripture, as Jesus leads the woman beyond her first literal understanding to an inner and spiritual understanding of what is actually happening. Further, he uses the moment to lead to an interfaith understanding too: "God is Spirit, and those who worship him will worship in Spirit and truth" (4:24).

The story exemplifies Jesus' noninterest in the religious culture and "denominationalism" of his own day. He not only talks to a strange woman alone (to the scandal of the disciples), but points out that the truth claims of both groups, Jews and Samaritans, are of no final interest to God: "The hour is coming when you will worship the Father neither here on this mountain nor in Jerusalem…authentic worshipers will worship the Father in Spirit and truth" (4:23); he repeats this twice, and the second time even more strongly (4:24). It is really quite amazing, and one wonders how we continue to defend such artificial divisions to this day, given this statement.

Of course, the whole point is that unless you experience the Spirit, which Jesus says is "the water that I will give which will turn into a spring within you, welling up unto eternal life" (4:14), the whole thing falls apart. If one has not made contact with the Spirit Spring of Water, we will always define ourselves by nonessentials and cultural accidents and external forms and formulas.

And then Jesus leads her to a sweeping and usually unnoticed concluding vision: "Open your eyes and see! The fields are shining for the harvest, the reaper can collect his wages *now*, the reaper can *already* bring in the grain of eternal life! The reaper and the sower can rejoice together" (4:35–36). You can hear Jesus' excitement at the possibilities. Why? Partly because it is all happening now! The word *already* or *now* is used three times in the passage, and the phrase "sower and reaper together" conflates any notion of time between action and reward. The sowing is the reaping.

You could also say that he is the reaper and she is the sower, and whatever is happening is happening right now. He has leapt beyond all boundaries of time, morality, and religion to announce a universal and gratuitous victory for God and for humanity that is taking place in the present tense (rather clear in verses 36–38)! This really is great stuff, which could still reform Christian pettiness and division, or any notion of the Gospel as a reward/punishment system that comes after death.

Today's Reading
Read the entire story of the Samaritan woman (John 4:1–42) in your preferred Bible. .

Starter Prayer
"God of Spirit and Truth, expand my mind, but even more my heart to receive your great and universal good news. I know that no change of heart happens without a change of mind, and no change of mind happens without a change of heart. Get me started in one place or the other!"

MONDAY OF THE THIRD WEEK OF LENT
Why Is My Group Always Better Than Your Group?

2 Kings 5:1–15b; Luke 4:24–30

Again, we are going to be exposed to two readings that utterly undercut our natural "groupishness"—two readings that laugh at our unwillingness to even *allow* God outside of our own assumptions, our tribe, and our definitions. The point is made so clearly in both that one wonders how we could have ever missed it.

The very telling First Reading from the second book of Kings sets up all the usual conflict (read "revelatory") situations. Let's list them here, and I think you can draw your own conclusion: There is Naaman (a Syrian commander), a leper, and not a Jew. A little slave girl is able to see where the spiritual power is and that it is to be found beyond their borders. Naaman wants the healing, but thinks money and his importance can buy it (later in verses 16–19 Elisha will refuse taking anything at all).

Naaman comes to the prophet Elisha's door, but then takes offense at the prophet himself who does not come out to meet him and at the prophet's insulting suggestion to bathe in the Jordan's miraculous waters instead of the waters of his own holy rivers in Syria. Naaman's own servants have to convince him to comply. Finally, he is fully cleansed and healed of his leprosy, but almost entirely in spite of himself! Talk about "amazing grace" being avoided. Talk about someone being healed while missing all the invitations and promises. Naaman is a complete victim of grace! It chooses him; he never really chooses it. He lives inside of a world of propriety and predictability, as many of us do. Yet a very humble God works anyway.

And it is to this obscure story that Jesus refers to point out to his contemporaries that the insider often misses the grace, while the outsider gets it. So much so that God can often only go to the outsider, "No prophet gains acceptance in his own place," he says. Then he points out that the prophet "Elijah was sent to the widow of Zarepath, a town in Sidon" (outside of Jewish territory). He more than suggests that it is often the outsider who crosses borders of prejudice to receive the gift, while you remain smugly inside your synagogues.

The ending is certain. "The whole audience in the synagogue was filled with indignation. They rose up and expelled him from the town, and led him to a cliff intending to hurl him over." We will "kill God" if he is not our God, and does not say it in our way, and inside of our group's language. Religion which was supposed to be life and healing for the world has too often become death and boundary-keeping for the few.

Today's Reading

Again, since the complete passages make the many points in full context, I ask you to read them for yourself in your Bible or Lectionary. Read 2 Kings 5:1–15 and Luke 4:24–30.

Starter Prayer

"God of Israel, Samaria, Sidon, and Syria, are you really all the same God? Can I allow you to be free, or should you follow our rules and our theology?"

TUESDAY OF THE THIRD WEEK OF LENT

Who Is in the Fiery Furnace and Who Is Not?

Daniel 3:25, 34–43; Matthew 18:21–35

Our First Reading today from the book of Daniel is from the prayer of one of the three young men in the fiery furnace. He is named Azariah ("God helps") and surely represents the desperate but fervent praying that would characterize anyone "walking around in the flames of a fiery furnace." He appeals to God to keep his part of the covenant relationship, with all of the proper humility, confession of sin, and pleading for mercy that might be expected. He asks Yahweh to operate from God's better, even best instincts, and assures Yahweh that they will do the same and "follow you with our whole heart" from now on. A good prayer that tells us about what we can expect from this God of Israel. They are in the furnace, but "the fire did not touch them or cause them any pain" (3:50).

The theme develops further in this allegorical Gospel story that is found only in Matthew. It is often called "the parable of the unforgiving debtor" which describes it rather well. As with so many parables, the opening question and the closing one-liner reveal the major point. It begins with Peter asking, "How many times must I forgive my brother [or sister]?" and Jesus answers that you must forgive them "seventy times seven!" In the in-between story, the Master is "moved with pity" and has cancelled the entire debt of a servant which would amount to nine million dollars! The parable ends with the invitational one-liner: "Each of you must forgive your brother [or sister] *from the heart!*" This is what the Master/God has just done.

The greedy and selfish debtor, who is owed a mere fifteen dollars, throttles his fellow servant, ignores his attempts and promises, and throws him into prison (as if that is going to help). And in his attempt to imprison the other, he ends up being "tortured" and imprisoned himself. This is a classic Middle Eastern wisdom story. It is both a gracious statement about what we can always expect from God and an honest warning about how any refusal to forgive actually destroys and imprisons the very one who refuses!

Jesus invites all of us in this rather easy-to-understand story into God's nonsensical loving "from the heart" which is the final staccato phrase. The connection I make between the two readings is that praying to forgive serious injuries is like praying while burning in a fiery furnace, and if you do not pray to be released from your unforgiving heart, *you* will indeed keep burning. Sometimes, only God can release you from such a furnace.

Today's Reading

"Do not let us be put to shame, but deal with us in your kindness and your great mercy. Deliver us by your wonders, and thus bring glory to your own name."

Daniel 3:42–43

"Should you not have dealt mercifully with your fellow servant just as I dealt with you?"

Matthew 18:33

Starter Prayer

"God of Compassion, Mother and Father of all Mercies, do not let us shame ourselves—or the wonder of your name—by living outside of the wondrous loop of your forgiveness and mercy."

WEDNESDAY OF THE THIRD WEEK OF LENT
Good Containers Are Necessary
Deuteronomy 4:1, 5—9; Matthew 5:17—19

The lesson I would like to
offer here is one of the most valuable, but also one of the hardest to
communicate to modern and postmodern Western people. We are all
descendants of the French and American Revolutions, which did not
have much use for "old" containers or even "containment" of any sort.
Americans call it "freedom," but we are going to see Jesus making the
case for a much older and biblical freedom than mere freedom from
restraints.

God is like an electric wire. You get burned if you make direct contact, or even if you assume that *you* have made direct contact! I am
speaking mythologically and psychologically here, where the pattern is
rather clear and often repeated. Jails and mental hospitals are filled
with people speaking directly for God, as are many churches for that
matter.

When Moses effusively praises the "statutes and the decrees" that
must be "observed," that must "not slip from your memory, but be
taught to your children's children," we educated and progressive types
just roll our eyes and wait for the next reading. But then we have Jesus,
who is seldom wrong but "might just be" in this case, saying that he has

no intention of "abolishing the law, or even the smallest letter of the law"—"until its purpose is achieved." What is going on here? We are not interested in going back to repressive and narrow notions of religion, are we? Maybe this can help:

Great Contents must be held by smaller holding tanks. There is really no other way, or we utterly inflate and destroy the human psyche and soul. It is only a very proud person, or a proud culture, who would think differently. You can only get Great Contents little by little, in stages and doses, when ready, and when you yourself are at the deeper levels. Otherwise, you always get burned! Laws, dogmas, even institutions, "statutes and decrees" are the necessary holding tanks, keeping you still and struggling in one place, until you can go deeper, and *know what they really mean!*

Or as Jesus says, "Until it has achieved its purpose" (in another translation, "until it all comes true"). Jesus knows that laws and dogmas are not goals or ends in themselves, and in that he disagrees with much immature religion, but *they are a necessary beginning point and holding tank—but one will invariably know that only later—when it all comes true!—and after the necessary struggle.* Great Things cannot fall into your little lap immediately, or they would not be Great Things.

Notice the word *until.* There is a point where many structures and verbalizations lose their importance, and even their helpfulness. As Paul will say later, they are only "nursemaids" (Galatians 3:24). I call them *training wheels*. Structures of various kinds are the wineskins, but are not the wine. They are the yeast, but not the dough. They are the first container, but not the final contents. But without the container, we invariably lose the essential contents.

Today's Readings

"What other nation has statutes and decrees that are as just as our whole law, which I am setting before you today?"

Deuteronomy 4:8

"I have come not to abolish the laws, but to fulfill them ["complete them," "bring them to perfection"].... Not the smallest letter of the law shall be done away with *until* it all comes true."

Matthew 5:17—18

Starter Prayer

"God of Law and God of Love, get me started, hold on fast to me, but also keep me going in the right direction, which is always toward you."

THURSDAY OF THE THIRD WEEK OF LENT

Driving Out Devils With Better-Disguised Devils

Jeremiah 7:23—28; Luke 11:14—23

In general, you tell people how to respond to you, and Jeremiah in the First Reading is setting himself, the people, and Yahweh up for a negative response. In being against "the devil," Jeremiah has become a bit of a devil himself. He condemns, fears, and scatters. He is a split and divided prophet at this point. This is surely what Paul later means when he says, "Prophesying is imperfect" (1 Corinthians 13:9). Jeremiah does eventually mature, but it takes a bit more suffering and failure to refine this "reluctant prophet," and there is still much failure to come in the rest of Jeremiah's life.

Jesus will carry this message further in the Gospel of Luke. He is doing good, driving the devil out of a man who cannot speak. One would think this would make the crowds happy, but they accuse him instead of having or even being a devil himself. When you try to fight evil, you are invariably accused of doing evil yourself. Isn't that interesting? And strange. Read history, and especially the lives of whistle-blowers, justice seekers, and peace workers. Maybe, in fact, this is what was happening to Jeremiah, and what is keeping him defensive in a corner.

At any rate, in this admittedly confusing text, Jesus variously defines himself as "not divided," "Someone Stronger," "the finger of God," "the Reign of God," and finally as "the one who gathers." He speaks from his inner identity and ground. He speaks from a "non-dual" place, his state of union with God, and real connection with the situation.

Note, however, that this is not just a "Look at what I can do" story. Jesus says we can "gather with him" in this way too (verse 23)! He always invites us in on his own victory. Whole people create whole people. Divided people heal nobody, but only scatter because they are "scattered" and un-whole themselves. They perpetuate the problem. Their motives, their loyalties, their identity, and their emotions are all over the place. The Greek word for devil is *diabolos*, which means split or divided, literally "thrown apart."

Jesus gathers and heals because he is one with himself, one with God, and even one with the pain of the man who cannot speak. He even wants to be one with the crowd. Predictably, however, his very wholeness divides Jesus the "Gatherer" from those who are scattered, and they accuse him of their own fault, which is "being a devil." For some reason, smug people are threatened by anyone farther along the path than they are. *When you actually fight real evil, you will invariably be accused of doing evil yourself.* Whereas, if you separate yourself from minor social "impurities," almost everyone will agree and jump on board. You see why we need deep discernment and real wisdom when it comes to the battle with evil.

Today's Reading

"The crowds were cynical and skeptical ['amazed']. Some of them said, 'It is by the prince of devils that he casts out devils'... Jesus said, 'When Someone Stronger comes along and overpowers the supposed strong man, he carries off the spoils. Anyone who is not 'one' will always be against me. Anyone who does not gather invariably scatters."

Luke 11:14—15, 22—23

Starter Prayer

"Warrior God, Crucified Christ, teach me how evil is really overcome. Do not let me be part of the problem, but the beginning myself of the answer."

FRIDAY OF THE THIRD WEEK OF LENT
The Two Loves Are Not Separate
Hosea 14:2—10; Mark 12:28—34

Our First Reading is the conclusion of the writings of the prophet Hosea. He taught an intimate, time-tried, and tender relationship with Yahweh, after experiencing God's own faithfulness to him. He was building on the cycles of give and take, faithfulness and unfaithfulness of his prostitute wife, Gomer—whom God told him to marry! His wife became the image of the soul before God. Think about that for a while. Just knowing Hosea's biography will allow you to read the text with new sympathy and impact. "I will always heal your disloyalty. I will love you freely with all my heart," says Yahweh, and that is how Hosea has come to love Gomer. We are not sure which came first, God's faithful love for Hosea or Hosea's forgiving love for Gomer.

In today's compelling Gospel, Jesus is putting together what he sees as the summit and the summary of his own Jewish teaching (from Deuteronomy and Leviticus), plus he might well be echoing a famous rabbi, Hillel, who was his contemporary. Hillel said to an overzealous young rabbinical student in Judea: *"What you find hateful do not do to another. This is the whole of the Law. Everything else is commentary. Now go learn that!"* One wonders if we do not still need to quote both Hillel and Jesus to overzealous theology majors and seminarians of all religions, even today!

The new message here is that Jesus combines the quote from Deuteronomy with the quote from Leviticus! The scribe has asked him for the "first and greatest" commandment, and Jesus gives him two commandments yet treats them as one! He connects two disparate passages and makes them one and the same, love of God and love of neighbor: "There is no commandment greater than *these!*" Matthew's telling makes it even more explicit, "And the second is just like it! On these two commandments hang everything in the law and in the prophets" (22:39–40). Hosea's love of Gomer and love of God are one and the same love. God's love of Gomer and of Hosea are one and the same love. If it is really Love, it is always One.

Happily, we have an enlightened seminary student in Mark's version, who not only fully affirms Jesus' teaching but adds, "This is far more important than any holocaust or sin offering." When one is being trained in "temple theology" or "priesthood" as a profession, this is all the more amazing and rare. Notice Jesus' strong validation of such "insight" or "wisdom" beyond his years: "You are not far from the Reign of God," young man! The passage ends by the crowd being utterly silenced by such clarity and simplicity.

Today's Reading

"'Listen, Israel, the Lord your God is One. You shall love the Lord with all your heart, with all your soul, with all your mind, and with all your strength.' And this is the second. 'You shall love your neighbor as you love yourself.' There is no commandment greater than these."

Mark 12:29–31

Starter Prayer

"One God, you make all things one. Even my own heart, and even one with the hearts of others, and most unbelievably one with yours."

SATURDAY OF THE THIRD WEEK OF LENT
The Illusion of "Sacrifice"
Hosea 6:1–6; Luke 18:9–14

Jesus himself quotes twice from this passage from Hosea in Matthew's Gospel, both times to defend himself from the "holier than thou" types: *"What God wants is merciful people, not heroic sacrifices, God wants you to know how love intimately works, and then you can skip your gestures of self-sacrifice"* (my paraphrase based on Hosea's own descriptions in 2:21ff and 8:11ff).

Jesus popularizes this somewhat neglected phrase in Hosea to defend himself from people who criticize him for consorting with sinners (Matthew 9:13), and again to defend his disciples and himself who are being criticized for not observing the Sabbath and feeding themselves (Matthew 12:7).

Both times he precedes it with a strong imperative or plea: "Go, learn the meaning of these words," or "If you only understood the meaning of these words." Well, it is still important that we learn the meaning of these words because much of religion has not. If we can get this, the Gospel of the publican and the Pharisee will quickly explain itself, and you will see that Jesus was an astute teacher, centuries ahead of modern psychology.

The Pharisee is the common heroic "sacrificer." People do not realize that this gesture largely feeds the ego and one's sense of self much more than anything else. *God does not need it. You need it.* Sacrifice is unconsciously an attempt to control God, who does much better without our control. "I fast twice a week, I pay tithes on all I possess.... I am not like the rest of men," he says. It looks like you are giving to God, country, church, the sports team, so all will undoubtedly admire you for it.

The social payoffs are so ego-inflating, there is no likelihood that "for God and country" thinking will diminish anytime soon. Sacrifice is often good and needed in life to help other people, but too often it is an attempt to build a more positive self-image by distinguishing oneself from others. Note his words, "I give you thanks, God, that I am not like the rest of men, grasping, crooked, and adulterous." Could the message be much clearer?

Our tax collector friend has apparently "gone and learned the meaning of the words" because from a distance with bowed head "All he did was beat his breast and say, 'God, be merciful to me, a sinner.'" And then Jesus delivers his stunning conclusion, still stunning today: "Believe me, this man went home from the temple justified before God, but the other did not." I hope you have observed that *Jesus is never upset at sinners! He is only upset with people who do not think they are sinners.* The

Pharisee is a public holy man who is not holy at all. The tax collector in Israel is a public sinner, with no credits to his name whatsoever, who ends up being the saint.

Today's Readings
"Go, learn the meaning of the words, what I want is mercy, not sacrifice, knowledge of God, not burnt offerings in the temple."

Hosea 6:6

"Jesus spoke this parable addressed to those who believed in their own moral superiority and who held everyone else in contempt. Two men went up to the temple to pray, one a Pharisee and the other a tax collector."

Luke 18:9—10

Starter Prayer
"Merciful God, all I can give you, and all you ever want, is who I really am. This little woman or little man that I am now gives you back my only and true self."

FOURTH SUNDAY OF LENT
Light Is About Seeing Correctly
1 Samuel 16:1b, 6–7, 10–13a; Ephesians 5:8–14; John 9:1–41

As the High Holy Days draw near, this Sunday of the "Second Scrutiny" of the catechumens revolved entirely around the theme of light and seeing things truthfully. This problem is at the heart of what almost all ancients saw as the "tragic sense of life." Our lack of self-knowledge and our lack of wisdom make humans do very stupid and self-destructive things. Because humans cannot see their own truth very well, they do not read reality very well either. We all have our tragic flaws and blind spots. Humans always need more "light" or enlightenment about themselves and about the endless mystery of God.

In the First Reading we have the prophet Samuel able to see what even David's father, Jesse, cannot see—that this youngest son of less lofty stature, forgotten out in the fields, is the chosen one. "Humans see only appearances, but God sees the heart," Samuel says. In the Second Reading from Ephesians, we have the text encouraging us to do our own "shadow work," and to bring our self-deceptions into the light. The catechumens were being encouraged to do a "fearless moral inventory," as the recovery movement would say today. Somewhere we must bring our shames and our denials into the light, or they kill us from within.

Finally, the great theater-piece Gospel is about a man born blind. Some think it was actually enacted in the sanctuary, with so many clear roles, interacting characters, and dramatic lines. We can only touch upon the surface here, but enough to point you beneath the surface, I hope. Let me list in quick succession the major themes so you cannot miss them:

- The "man born blind" is the archetype for all of us at the beginning of life's journey.
- The moral blame game as to why or who caused human suffering is a waste of time.
- The man does not even ask to be healed. It is just offered and given.
- Religious authorities are often more concerned about control and correct theology than actually healing people. They are presented as narrow and unloving people throughout the story.
- Many people have their spiritual conclusions before the facts in front of them. He is a predefined "sinner" and has no credibility for them.
- Belief in and love of Jesus come *after* the fact, subsequent to the healing. Perfect faith or motivation is not always a prerequisite for God's action. Sometimes God does things for God's own purposes.
- Spirituality is about seeing. Sin is about blindness, or as Saint Gregory of Nyssa will say, "Sin is always a refusal to grow."
- The one who knows little, learns much (what we call "beginner's mind") and those who have all their answers already, learn nothing.

Today's Reading

"I do not know whether [Jesus] is a sinner or not, I only know this much, I was once blind, and now I see."

John 9:25

"I came into the world to divide it, to make the sightless see and to reveal to those who think they see it all that they are blind."

John 9:39

Starter Prayer

"God of all Light and Truth, just make sure that I am not a blind man or woman. Keep me humble and honest, and that will be more than enough work for you."

MONDAY OF THE FOURTH WEEK OF LENT
Could the "New" Thing Be Inclusion?
Isaiah 65:17–21; John 4:43–54

There is not a clear and evident connection between the two readings today, just plenty of opportunities for the reader and the preacher to make the connections themselves. Let's try this one. Most of us have been led to believe that prophets "foretell" the future. That is true, and it is also misleading. It is not the point here. Prophets are seers of the big patterns; they see what is always and forever true. Prophets like Isaiah know how God acts by watching and listening, and they have no doubt about the "meta-narratives," the Real Story that is always going on inside of our little stories. One of the big patterns is that God's message always gets wider and more universal, despite our best attempts to limit it.

So when Third Isaiah talks about Yahweh creating "new heavens and a new earth" and "delight" and "rejoicing," the passing away of "weeping and crying," or the extended life of a man, he is not so much talking about concrete particulars as he is talking about universals, the big things that are always true, and might also be true here or there. It seems that ancient peoples had a larger sense of history and truth than we do. Maybe they were just more patient in seeing the big patterns unfold.

So when we have Jesus come back to Galilee, the first new thing is that he is accosted by a "royal official" who wants a miracle for his dying son. Now for a non-Jew of the "nobility" to trust an itinerant Jewish healer with no formal credentials is certainly a breakthrough into newness. The official trusts Jesus at his word, with no evidence at hand. When the official returns home, his weeping is indeed turned into delight, and we have one of the few examples of non-local healing in Jesus' ministry. There is no mention whatsoever of any checklist of beliefs, no correct loyalty systems, no asking whether the royal official is in his first marriage, or whether he has made a good confession of his sins. It seems really rather irresponsible of Jesus.

The whole story seems to be an illustration of the opening line, "A prophet gets no respect from his own" (John 4:44), who are often asking the wrong questions, it seems. As it comes to be expected in the Gospels, it is the outsider who invariably "gets it," while the insiders will largely continue to fight him, as they defend much smaller truths. The circle of the biblical revelation keeps widening to create that "new earth" of Isaiah, and within a century a people who will call themselves *catholic* or universal. Here comes everybody! One wonders how we ever made religion into any kind of exclusionary system whatsoever when the vast majority of Jesus' healings seem to happen to the excluded ones and maybe even the unworthy ones.

Today's Readings

"The things of the past shall not be remembered or come to mind. Instead there shall always be rejoicing and happiness in what I create."

Isaiah 65:17–18

"The man put his trust in the word that Jesus had spoken to him, and set off for home.... He and his whole household thereupon became believers."

John 4:50, 53

Starter Prayer

God of all names and all love, give us hearts to include all that you are willing to include, to forgive all that you so easily forgive, and to join you in doing something truly "new" on this earth.

TUESDAY OF THE FOURTH WEEK OF LENT
The Soul Needs Images and Imaging to "Know" Things

Ezekiel 47:1–9, 12; John 5:1–16

Human lives are made of moments, incidents, happenings, and what become anecdotal events, some of which we generalize about and make into full "belief systems." Art, pictures, snapshot biographies, metaphors, and stories have the ability to do this very *quickly and deeply* for us. They touch and gather the unconscious much more than concepts do. Once we can coalesce our varied experiences into a "picture," it has much more power for us to either heal us or hurt us or at least change us. The Bible, of course, is hoping to present us with some healing stories and images that allow us to reconfigure our life in God and in truth.

One of those deeply healing metaphors is water, and we see it in both readings today. Ezekiel presents water flowing from every side of the temple as the source of life, endless fertility: all living creatures, fish, and trees "whose fruit shall serve for food, and their leaves for medicine." What an excellent image of Divine abundance and the universal flourishing that comes from it!

In John's Gospel we see another image of fruitful and healing water, fittingly called Bethesda or "house of mercy." Now we have the healing waters available and bubbling, a house of mercy for sure, but a man who is right there not making use of it! He is paralyzed as much in spirit as in his body. This is the real "sin" and tragedy that he must be healed of. He is playing the victim, "I have no one to plunge me into the pool. By the time I get there someone else has always beaten me to it." And he has been saying this for thirty-eight years!

So Jesus orders him up, and tells him to pick up his mat and walk for himself. Jesus mirrors his best self for the man, he empowers him, and gives him back his own power, he "images" him, he gives the man back to himself by giving him *His self*. This is the way it has to happen, because we all begin to see ourselves as other people see us—for good and for ill. With Jesus, it is always for good, but such perfect mirroring also carries further relationship and responsibilities with it.

He warns the man not to turn back to his paralysis, "or something worse will overtake you." This "regressive restoration of the old persona" is a very common pattern when we are sent out into new and risky worlds when we have to take responsibility for ourselves, when we must courageously face our own lives and stand on our own courageous feet. There are few honest guides, like Jesus, at this point. Most will tell you to "take good care of yourself" and pad your false self. Jesus never does that.

Such regressive restoration of persona commonly happens to both individuals, and also to institutions, as we continually see in our country, our social groups, and even more sadly in our churches. They too often go back to nostalgia for the past and victimhood for the future in lieu of courage or guidance. We need healing images and courageous people to image us at our best. Nothing else will invite us into the flowing waters from the temple and the always bubbling pool of divine mercy. Many never take the risk, and remain spiritual infants even much beyond "thirty-eight years."

Today's Readings

"He made me wade through the water, which was now knee deep. Again he measured off a thousand cubits and made me wade again, and the water was up to my waist."

Ezekiel 47:4

"Do you want to be healed?…Then stand up, pick up your mat and walk!"

John 5:7, 9

Starter Prayer

"Healing God, give me the courage to move forward, and help me to see that my deepest sin might be my unwillingness to keep growing."

WEDNESDAY OF THE FOURTH WEEK OF LENT
The Two-Way Mirror
Isaiah 49:8–15; John 5:17–30

The First Reading is one
of the most lovely in all of Isaiah, and its metaphors make some think
that Second Isaiah might well have been a woman.

It has a delicacy of expression that feels more like Julian of Norwich
or Thérèse of Lisieux than any bearded prophet. She invites those
imprisoned to "come out" and makes it safe for those in dark interiors
to "show themselves." By the end, we are surely ready to be held by God
in the way that a mother remembers "tenderly" what was once in her
womb. Again, as yesterday, we have healing images and imaging going
on in both texts.

It continues in John's Gospel. In fact we have several mirrorings
going on here, and one false one that is warned against: (1) Jesus feels
himself mirrored by God, "The Father goes on working, and so do I,"
and he even "dares to speak of God as his own Father" and "equal,"
which deeply upsets the religious establishment. (2) Then we have
"the Son" mirroring us, the readers, and "granting life to those he
wishes." He is the two-way mirror looking in both directions, as it
were. (3) We also have God refusing to mirror us negatively, "The
Father judges no one," and the Son passing it on and allowing the

reader to "bypass condemnation" and "pass from death to life" now. The message has met its mark and its mirror. The transformative imaging has been passed to us, and now we must not condemn because we have not been condemned.

I know there are several passages in this text that appear to be threatening us with judgment or condemnation, and unfortunately that is all that fear types will hear or remember. But if you read the entire text as a whole, and in the light of the primal and positive mirroring of God, Jesus being the two-way mirror in between (to "honor the Son" is to receive his passing on of the divine image), you will see that the real import is that *each of us is our own truthful judge and our own best friend* if we but look honestly into the perfect and compassionate Divine Mirror, mirrored to us by Jesus, the Son. (A bit of advice: Use the word *mirrored* every time you read the word *judgment* in the Bible, and you will come much closer to the truth.)

Today's Readings

"He who pities them, leads them, and guides them beside springs of water.... Can a mother forget her infant, or be without tenderness for the child of her womb? Even if she could, I will never forget you."

Isaiah 49:10, 15

"I do not do anything of myself. I judge as I hear, and my judgment is true, because I am not seeking my own will, but the will of the One who sent me."

John 5:30

Starter Prayer
"God of the judgment I once feared, you have now drawn close to me like a mother. As a child does at the breast, I find myself delighting in your own delighting and delightful face."

THURSDAY OF THE FOURTH WEEK OF LENT
Cosmic Courtroom Scenes
Exodus 32:7–14; John 5:31–47

In both readings today we have "Reality" put on trial, and in both cases Reality/God wins. In the book of Exodus, just after the golden calf experience, Yahweh is calling the people of Israel to account, and Moses becomes their lawyer and defense attorney. He reminds God of their past history together and tells God in effect to be true to himself and to his promises. Yahweh relents, after having started this tirade telling Moses these are "your people"! Sounds like an exasperated parent in conflict with the kids!

The wonderful thing about such Jewish Scriptures as these is that it presents God as relational, able to be influenced and changed, a God of give and take, which becomes the "personal" notion of God that we have in Judeo-Christianity to this day. It lays the ground for love, freedom, and actual relationship, instead of just fate, unchangeable law, and inevitability. The secret in biblical prayer is always to expect God to be true to God's own name, identity, and patterns of goodness in the past, and not just begging God to conform to my immediate ego needs. Prayer, more than anything, seeks, creates, and preserves relationship—which is always both giving and receiving. Here it is mostly receiving.

Then in a somewhat labored but significant Gospel, John has Jesus on trial before the religious authorities, largely as his own defense attorney. He has no Moses to do this job, but he first appeals to John the Baptist as his star witness. Then he appeals to "the works that I do" as fitting evidence, then to God the Father "whom they cannot hear," next to their own Scriptures "in which you assume you have eternal life," and finally Jesus says that Moses will be their accuser because they do not believe him either. All in all, it is a full rout against all dishonest religion. He defeats them by their own criteria, yet it still does not work.

His explanation of their blindness is found between verses 41–44 where he points out that they are caught up in what French philosopher René Girard would call "mimetic rivalry," the human world of comparison, competition, and imitation. Inside that blind and incestuous loop of mutual approval and back scratching, God can never be found. Great spiritual truth must always be known in a "vertical" way, as it were, and not through the horizontal knowings of the always lazy and fearful collective, usually still in the first half of life awareness: "What everybody says and thinks" is its usual and standard form. Here mass consciousness and group pressure substitute for any real or necessary encounter with the Holy.

Jesus sets himself free in this courtroom scene by resetting the bar and revealing their unwillingness to make honest use of their own witnesses and their own internal evidence. He clearly wins, but there is no one there to congratulate him. He is a second half of life man in a first half of life religious courtroom.

Today's Reading

"As for human approval, this means nothing to me.... How can people like you believe, when you look to one another for validation, and are not concerned with the validation that comes from the one God?"

John 5:41, 44

Starter Prayer

"Just God, if you are the judge, then I will happily accept your witnesses, your evidence, and your conclusions. Because I always know that your only criterion is to be true to yourself, and you are infinite Love and Mercy."

FRIDAY OF THE FOURTH WEEK OF LENT

The Demonization of the Threatening "Other"

Wisdom 2:1a, 12–22; John 7:1–2, 10, 25–30

We have perhaps read the studies which show that once a group has decided to differentiate itself from another group, the rules of conversation change toward that group. We are inclined to believe the worst of them, paranoia and conspiracy theories soon abound, they are fair game for the commentators, and our chosen mistrust looks for any justification whatsoever to fear, hate, or even kill. Soon any defensive or even offensive attacks toward that person or group are fully rationalized and justified. It is a rare person who can stand uninfluenced by this field of gossip and innuendo. This is the sad pattern of human history.

It is just such an atmosphere that is presented in both readings today, as we near the climactic events of Holy Week. The taunting verses from the book of Wisdom sound familiar to most Christians because they are the backdrop of the Crucifixion scene: "If he is the son of God, then God will defend him." In the full text we read a kind of bravado and defiance, daring the "just person" to prove himself. It feels like the school bully mocking the classmate who might be smarter, more popular, or even more mature. For some strange reason, fearful humans are threatened by anyone outside of their frame of reference. They are always a threat and must be brought down.

The same pattern is then found in the Gospel. So strange that even religious authorities can speak openly of wanting to kill Jesus, and the crowds even openly know about this. What has religion come to? Vengeance is often an open, but denied secret when fear and gossip reign in a society. Every attempt is being made to discredit Jesus, and even his family of origin, which is a very common pattern. (The whole of John 7 might give you even more of the feeling of malice and intrigue than the selected passage here in the Lectionary.)

Jesus is slowly being isolated for the attack, he moves around "secretly." You can feel his loneliness and anguish, and all he can do is claim his true origins—to deaf ears. In these days, we are being invited to share in the passion of Jesus, and in the aloneness and fear of all who have been hated and hunted down since the beginning of time.

Today's Readings

"Let us beset the just one, because he is obnoxious to us, he sets himself against our doings.... To us he is the censure of our thoughts. Merely to see him is a hardship."

Wisdom 2:12, 14

"[Jesus] had decided not to travel in Judea because some of the Jews were looking for a chance to kill him.... Some of the people of Jerusalem remarked 'Is this not the one they want to kill?'"

John 7:1, 25

Starter Prayer
"God of loving truth, keep me from the world of gossip and accusation. Do not let me 'kill' others, even in my mind or heart."

SATURDAY OF THE FOURTH WEEK OF LENT

All Controversies Can Be Resolved by an Appeal to Authority

Jeremiah 11:18−20; John 7:40−53

The noose tightens as we come into the final weeks of Lent. As people become more afraid and insecure, they do not know how to access their own soul, move to prayer, or toward their better instincts. At that point, the easy and comforting response is to quote some Scripture, some authority, or some legal principle. It takes away one's anxiety rather quickly. The fundamentalist is more than anything else *one who believes that all problems can be resolved by an appeal to authority.* No inner life is necessary, no faith journey, no actual experience; someone else can do all my homework for me. "I do not need to take responsibility for my own life, someone higher will," they seem to say.

This theme is most obvious in the Gospel, since the First Reading from Jeremiah, although touching, reveals him back into righteous and divine vengeance against others. We are so tired of this, but I would probably be the same if I were under attack as much as Jeremiah was.

In the Gospel passage today we have nothing but arguments about authority and "Who are you loyal to?"—Who do you follow or believe?

Which is the correct Scripture? What is the proper interpretation of that Scripture? What group do you represent? Are you loyal to us or to Galilee? It is all about loyalty tests and reassurance of my fears and doubts. Human blindness and prejudice make you want to cry; and sadly, the patterns never change in politics, religion, or culture to this day.

Each remains smug and ignorant "*in his own house,*" as the episode sadly concludes: "Don't bother me with larger wisdom, I have my small truth," they seem to say. I so sincerely wish it were that easy. Now no one has to read or see what is right in front of them, as they are each hidden in their own house and quoting their own authorities. So read the full text of the Gospel now, but even more, the text of what is right in front of us today, the patterns of tabloid journalism, gossip, and condemnation by spin or sarcasm, that are the very shape of the world that we live in.

Today's Reading
"You do not see any of the Sanhedrin believing in him, do you? Or the Pharisees? Only this lot that knows nothing about the law—and they are lost anyway!... And each went off to his own house."

John 7:48, 52

Starter Prayer
"God of All Authority, I place my trust in you, which is often to feel alone and without reassurance on this earth."

FIFTH SUNDAY OF LENT
What Is Life and What Is Death?
John 11:1–45

Humans are the only crea-
tures who have knowledge of their own death. Its awareness creeps up
on us as we get older. All other animals, plants, and the cycles of nature
themselves seem to live out and surrender to the pattern of mortality.
This places humans in a state of anxiety and insecurity from our early
years. We know on some level that whatever this is that we are living
will not last. This changes everything, probably more than we realize
consciously. So our little bit of consciousness makes us choose to be
unconscious. It hurts too much to think about it.

On this last Sunday before Palm Sunday, we dare to look at the "last
enemy," death. And the only way we can dare to part the curtain and
view death is to be told about our resurrection from it! Yet, I assume
we all know that Lazarus did eventually die. Maybe ten years later,
maybe even twenty, but it did happen, we assume. What then is the
point of this last dramatic "sign" before Jesus' own journey toward
death?

An important clue is given right before the action, when the disciples
try to discourage Jesus from going back to Judea where he is in danger.
Jesus says calmly, "Are there not twelve hours in the day? When a

person can walk without stumbling? When he sees the world bathed in light." Jesus refuses to fear darkness and death. Quickly he adds, "Our friend Lazarus is sleeping, I am going to wake him" (John 11:9–11).

Those who draw upon the twelve hours, who see the world bathed in light now, have begun to see the pattern. As is often the case with wise people, they let "nature nurture them." Yes, the other hours of darkness will come, a metaphor for death, but now we know that it will not last. It is only a part, but not the whole of life—just as the day itself is twelve hours and night is the other twelve, two sides of the one mystery of Life. Jesus' job is simply to "wake" us up to this, as he did Lazarus and the onlookers. Once you are awake to the universal truth, then physical death is no enemy to be feared. "Do you believe this?" he says (11:26).

And then in a final brilliant finale to the story, *he invites the onlookers to join him in making resurrection happen:* "Move the stone away!... Unbind him, and let him go free!" It seems that we have a part to play in creating a culture of life and resurrection. We must unbind one another from our fears and doubts about the last enemy, death. We must now "see that the world is bathed in light" and allow others to enjoy the same seeing—through our lived life. The stone to be moved is always our fear of death, the finality of death, any blindness that keeps us from seeing that death is merely a part of the Larger Mystery called Life. It does not have the final word.

Today's Reading

"'This sleep is not to end in death, but is instead to reveal the glory of God'.... With a sigh that came straight from the heart...He cried out in a loud voice, 'Move the stone away!... Lazarus, come forth!'... 'Now, you unbind him and let him go free.'"

John 11:4, 34, 38, 43–44

Starter Prayer

"Good God, the creator of light and darkness, You who move the sun and the stars, move us into the place of light, a light so large that it will absorb all the darkness."

MONDAY OF THE FIFTH WEEK OF LENT
Lust and Love
Daniel 13:1—9, 15—17, 19-30, 33—62; John 8:1—11

In the seminary these readings were always wonderfully challenging for us celibates. We would watch our professors twitch with discomfort as we read publicly in church of a naked woman bathing, open voyeurism, lustful elders who told bold lies to cover their sin and to condemn innocent Susanna. "Bring me oil and soap," said Susanna to the maids, "and shut the garden door while I bathe." Little did she know that there were dirty old men hiding behind the bushes.

The wise celebrant of the day invariably encouraged that we use the shorter version of the reading. So we went back to our rooms and checked out the full thirteenth chapter of the book of Daniel. We felt sorry for the poor Protestants who had excised this from the official canon and even called it "apocrypha." This was good—bad—stuff!

But it was fortunately followed by the wonderful Gospel about the adulterous woman, who is caught and yet freed. In Scripture class it became apparent that this story was rather clearly "inserted" into John 8, since it does not follow from, nor lead to, the texts before or after, and it is not found in the earliest manuscripts. All agree today that it is canonical, and perhaps actually from Luke in another place, and we are very glad it is official biblical text, for the message is superb and needed.

We are all nervous, confused, and guilt-ridden about sex, almost more than anything else. It is what C.G. Jung would call a "complex"— various thoughts or images which hold all kinds of strong and unconscious energy, flowing out in irrational directions. Our reactions are always strange and confused when we are in the grip of a complex, whether it be overly positive or overly negative. We surely see it here in both readings today.

In short, humans have a hard time distinguishing between lust and true love. For most men, it takes much of our lives to know the difference, and we have just such men illustrated in both readings today— and two women the worse for it. Although a dozen needed sermons could come from this Gospel, may it suffice here to highlight one line in our reading that might be the most quoted verse from Jesus, and spoken here in defense of the woman.

If you will allow me one further interpretation, I personally think that Jesus' bending down to write on the ground (the only example of Jesus writing) was to avoid any confrontational stare and cruel accusation of the men. He wanted them to take responsibility themselves. His love was so gracious and universal that he even wanted to save them from the condemnation of his eyes: "Neither do I condemn you," he says *to both the woman and the men.* This is another example of his wonderful "third-way" solutions.

Today's Reading
"If there is one of you who has not sinned, let him be the first to throw the stone. Then he bent down and began to write on the ground."

John 8:7–8

Starter Prayer
"God of love, you made love so important for our salvation, that you took the risk of us doing it poorly, as we all do. Keep us free from throwing stones at others, so we can see our own clumsy attempts at divine love."

TUESDAY OF THE FIFTH WEEK OF LENT
Spiritual Vaccination
Numbers 21:4−9; John 8:21−30

We have all seen the rod of Asclepius, or its common variation, the caduceus, on medical insignia throughout the world. It was the symbol of this Greek god of healing, but is also found here in our First Reading from the book of Numbers (21:4−9). It is a single or double serpent winding around a pole, and we are not sure if the Greeks or the Hebrews had it first. But surely its meaning was a universal discovery that today we would perhaps call vaccination! In short, "the cause is also the cure"! Who would have thought? It seems to be true both medically and psychologically.

At any rate, we have Moses prescribing such medicine to the complaining Hebrews in the desert, who were being bit by winged/fiery serpents. For some reason, he tells them to make a bronze version of the same and put it on a standard, which is perhaps unlikely considering their prohibition against idols. But he said, "If anyone is bitten and looks on it, they shall live." Apparently, it worked, to their healing and our embarrassment.

The meaning and healing symbol returns again in John's Gospel on many levels, all of them significant. The recurring phrase is, "the lifted up one." It has now become a rallying cry for the Jesus who was raised up on the cross and thus "vaccinated us against" doing the same (3:13 and 19:37). Jesus being "lifted up" is offered as a healing icon of love to all of history (12:32), and finally, as a victory sign of the final resurrection and ascension of all the human ones, as is prefigured in today's account about the archetypal "Human One," Jesus (8:28).

This is powerful material, just as vaccinations always are. The crucified Jesus is God's at least three-level vaccination plan: (1) *against* humanity's desire to scapegoat or kill, (2) *so we could "catch"* a universal and healing love from God, and (3) *toward* the mutual encounter whereby we know the great "I AM" through our own deepest "I am."

In each case, we have a Divine Medicine brought down to a small but potent dosage so we can handle it and *it can handle us!* That is what true spiritual symbols always do. Remember what we said earlier in Lent: Any direct contact with God is like contact with an electric wire—it burns you unless you have some good filters and a very humble humanity to receive it.

No wonder so many Catholics and Orthodox never tired of hanging images of the crucified Jesus in their homes and in their churches. We needed to "lift up" and "gaze upon" the transformative image just as Moses first did in the desert. It can and did and will change many lives and much of history.

Today's Reading

"'You belong to what is below. I belong to what is above. You belong to this world, the world which cannot hold me' ["handle"?].... So they said, 'Who are you?'... 'When you lift up the Son of Man you will gradually realize that I AM, and that I do nothing by myself.'"

John 8:23, 25, 28

Starter Prayer

"Dear and Divine Physician, I need all of the medicine you are willing to offer me. Give me what I can handle, when I can handle it, and may I let you be the Handler."

WEDNESDAY OF THE FIFTH WEEK OF LENT
A Prior State of Hostility Will Distort Everything
Daniel 3:14–20, 91–92; John 8:31–42

We have all experienced it. When someone wants to dislike us, no matter what we do, it will be interpreted in the worst possible fashion. As we often say, "You can't win." When someone's heart is hardened already, you could be Jesus himself, and they will seriously see you as wrong, inferior, dangerous, and heretical—which is what is about to happen in Holy Week.

At that point, no matter what evil a person decides to do to you, it will be deemed virtuous and praiseworthy by hardened or paranoid people in the hostile camp. "He is a terrorist!" they might say. Never having the humility or honesty to admit that to someone else, looking from a different perspective (which is deemed totally wrong), he probably looks like a sacrificial and dedicated freedom fighter. Well, this is exactly what is happening in both readings today.

In the book of Daniel, we have old king Nebuchadnezzar's "face livid with utter rage" at three poor little Jewish boys with strange names— just because they will not "worship the golden statue that I set up." Do you hear that? Who made it golden and who set it up? Could it be

Nebuchadnezzar himself? What a perfect metaphor for total and absolute narcissism. Poor Shadrack, Meshach, and Abednego are dealing with an already closed and self-enclosed system. Nothing can get in or out of this king's heart or head. It is no surprise that he has to throw them into the white-hot furnace. There is no other way he can retain his "truth," which, of course, is no truth at all.

Then we have a very complex Gospel text, which does not present "the Jews" in a very good light. John had to make a clear villain here for the sake of the debate, so he safely chose his own race and people. There are claims and counterclaims of truth, freedom, lineage, tradition, killing, and divine illegitimacy. Jesus fights back well, but he does not have a chance. Their hearts are already hardened in place, which in this archetypal story is really not a statement about Jews as much as it is about all of humanity. "I have my conclusions already, do not bother me with any new information that might make me change my judgment."

Most Christians would probably be slow to admit that by these criteria almost all of us would have opposed Jesus. "This is not our tradition, he is not from our group, and he has no credentials!"

Today's Reading

"If you make my word your home, you will know the truth, and the truth will set you free. 'We are descendants of Abraham and have never

been the slaves to anyone! What do you mean by "'We will be fr
Jesus answered them, 'I tell you sincerely, anyone who chooses a dead-
ended life and stops growing, is in sin, and that is slavery.'"

John 8:31–35

Starter Prayer
"God of perfect freedom, open spaces inside of our minds, our hearts,
and our memories, so we can just begin to be free. Do not let me be
hardened against anyone of your creatures, so that I cannot hear and
respect their truth."

THURSDAY OF THE FIFTH WEEK OF LENT
All Glory Is Reflected Glory
Genesis 17:3–9; John 8:51–59

In the First Reading from Genesis, we have an encounter between Yahweh and Abraham, when he is ninety-nine years old. It is a third-time repeat of his first call, each time adding a few new elements to the meaning of their relationship or "covenant." But one thing that does not change is that although the relationship is totally initiated and invited from God's side, it is still a bilateral covenant. There is always a bit more of a requirement expected from Abraham each time: leaving his country and family (12:1–2), the sacrifice of animals (15:9–11), and here there will be required circumcision (17:9–14), and belief that he will have a son (17:16ff). At which both he and his wife, Sarah, laugh!

The God-human relationship must start bilaterally. It is the only way to get us into the boxing ring. *It is the only way to hold us still in one place long enough—so the beginnings of the give-and-take of relationship can happen.* But it is not the final goal. Many, if not most, never get beyond "religion as requirements." What does your religion require of you? Is that wrong in your denomination? It is the question of the rich young man, "What must I do to inherit eternal life?" Since all human relationships are bilateral (least of all, the parent-child), we tend to structure all of our experiences that way. In other words, we are almost totally unprepared for God! Unless we know how a perfect parent might love a child—unilaterally

Gradually, as the Hebrew people are continually unfaithful to the initial Abrahamic Covenant, we will see that it becomes more and more unilateral from Yahweh's side. Really quite wonderful! God does it all, whether or not we cooperate at all. I would not believe it myself if I did not read the successive covenants with Noah, David, and, of course, what Jeremiah predicts, and we eventually call "the new covenant" with Jesus. Each succeeding time God, in effect, says *"I might as well let you in on the big secret, I do it all anyway!"* Jesus becomes the living icon of that new and everlasting covenant, where God does all the loving and we do all the receiving. It is symbolized every time we hand out the "cup of his blood" to you—and say "the new and everlasting covenant."

This gives you a foundation and background with which to read the Gospel today. Jesus himself stands in right relationship with his Father and receives all his "glory" from him. It is a fully reflected glory and therefore unwavering, constant, infinite, and from one Source. This is exactly the "eternal life" that he speaks of here, and then even tells us we can have it too. So you see the sequencing: Jesus perfectly reflects God's glory given from the Father, then we are invited to receive and reflect that same glory which is reflected from Jesus. *It is all a reflection received, a glory given, inherent, and unilateral gift from God's side.* (Remember, we are not talking about psychological or moral worthiness here, we are talking about metaphysical identity, our True Self, which is our "birthright" from God.) We humans are always unwhole, but we still receive and can ever more perfectly reflect our divine identity in God.

This is the great I AM, which Jesus claims at the very end of today's Gospel (8:58), and yet because they refuse to see it in themselves or in him, they "throw rocks at him." It is not just hating him but is an expression of their own self-hatred. Read the passage below, which is so central and crucial for our understanding, that I will add my commentary within the text:

Today's Reading

"If I glorify myself, that glory means nothing [Eternal life is not self generated]. He who gives me the glory is the Father, the very one you claim for your God [It is a mere verbal affirmation]. But you do not know him ["You do not allow or trust the reflection of God's glory in yourself"]. But I know him ["I allow and believe the reflection fully"]. If I said I do not know him, I would be no better than you—a liar!" [Jesus is not being cruel here. He is saying that they are telling an *untruth* by denying their divine identity. We *do* know him, reflect him, and even have eternal life now, but we refuse to see it, and in that sense, we are all "liars."]

John 8:51, 54–55

Starter Prayer

"My God, this changes everything. Let it be true for me. Let me see what you saw. Allow me to know that I and all of us are reflections of the Eternal Glory."

Words Are Necessarily Dualistic; Experience Is Always Non-Dual

Jeremiah 20:10–13; John 10:31–42

These parallel readings today will allow me to illustrate what I think is central to religion's best instincts and also allows religious people to make their worst mistakes. We all confuse words with reality itself, and this still happens among people who believe that in Jesus "The Word became flesh, and lives among us." We *should* know better.

In the First Reading from the reluctant prophet Jeremiah, we see him in a moment of real paranoia, "All those who were my friends are waiting for any mistake of mine. 'Perhaps he will trap himself in his words, and then we can prevail,'" they say. If you continue, you will see that Jeremiah soon becomes as bad as they are. He asks God to wreak vengeance on them, humiliate them with "unforgettable disgrace," and even adds, "Let me watch it!" This is not a highly inspired or inspiring text, but all fear, righteousness, and vengeance in the name of God. Jeremiah becomes here what he hates and fears in others.

In the Gospel we have Jesus also being attacked and about to be stoned for "making himself God." And instead of denying the claim, he invites them into the same experience, by quoting Psalm 82:6: "Is it not written in your law, 'I said, you are gods!' And this is spoken to those to whom God's word is addressed, and Scripture cannot be rejected. So why do you claim that I blaspheme?" This is a daring and non-dualistic acclamation from Jesus! He simply shouts out his own divine union and invites them to the same experience, "I am in the Father and the Father is in me" (10:38), as he stands before them by all visible evidence, a human being just as they are! "Yes, I claim it, but we all can!" he seems to say. The invitational message is clear and compelling, but it cannot be heard through words, for some reason. It is, quite literally, too good to be true. It can only be experienced. So they "try to arrest him," just as much of Christian history has arrested, feared, and denied any message of actual union with God.

Today's Reading

"It is not for any good deed that we are stoning you," the Jews said, "but for blaspheming. You are clearly only a man, and yet you make yourself a God.... 'Why do you say I am blaspheming, because I say that I am God's son?'"

John 10:33, 36

Starter Prayer

"Good and Generous God, why do you have such a hard time giving yourself away? You want to share your very self with us, your own divine nature, and we will not allow it."

SATURDAY OF THE FIFTH WEEK OF LENT
True Unity and False Unity
Ezekiel 37:21–28; John 11:45–56

Our two readings today give us a chance to illustrate a rather important spiritual point: There is a good way to create unity and there is a bad way.

In the First Reading from Ezekiel, Yahweh tells the prophet to perform a ritual that would mimic what God wants to do. Yahweh has just told Ezekiel to take two sticks, and write on each of them: on one stick, "Judah and those loyal to him," and on the other, "Ephraim and those loyal to him" (37:16). These were, of course, the two kingdoms of Israel, and Yahweh tells him to "hold the two pieces of wood in your hand where you can see it" (37:20). Hold the two small loyalty systems into one larger unity as it were. Today we might call it "positive imaging!"

Our Lectionary text today begins at this point, and Yahweh promises to "gather" the two kingdoms into one, "rescue" them, "cleanse" them, and make with them "a covenant of peace." "My dwelling shall be with them. I will be their God, and they shall be my people" (37:26–27). A magnificent passage portraying how God unites, by the positive energy of loving, "shepherding," and revealing the Divine Presence in one's midst and between them. This is the good way, God's way to create unity.

Then in the Gospel, since we are about to enter Holy Week tomorrow, we are exposed to the much more common way that cultures try to create unity, what René Girard calls "the negative unanimity around one." You can either rally around love to unite, or you can rally around fear, gossip, paranoia, and negativity, usually symbolized by one issue or person. I am afraid the second rallying point is the much more common. It is more efficient and gathers groups much more quickly and tightly than love does. I wish it were not true.

In this case, the rallying cry is the killing of Jesus. He is the "one" around which they can become "one." This is supported by the high priest, Caiaphas, in the name of what we would now call "the national security state" (see verses 48–50), and as always, it works. The drama is now set for Holy Week. The scapegoat to create unity has been chosen. *Little do they know that another Deeper Unity will also be set into motion that continues to this day.* There are still two ways of gathering, the way of fear and hate and the way of love. But do not yourself be afraid, because Jesus is still "gathering." God's continual job description, it seems, is mimed in the two bound sticks of Ezekiel. God is always and forever making one out of two.

Today's Reading

"Can you not see that it is better for you to have one man die for the people, than to have the whole nation destroyed? He did not say this on his own. It was rather as high priest that he prophesied that Jesus would die for the nation—and not for this nation only, but to gather into one all the dispersed children of God."

John 11:50–52

Starter Prayer

"Jesus, our Scapegoat, you forever show us on the cross both the human problem and the divine solution. Help me to be part of your solution and to stop creating and persecuting scapegoats. I now know that I might just be killing you."

Holy Week

.   .   .

PALM SUNDAY
Waxing and Waning
Philippians 2:6–11

In this overflow of rich themes today, including an entire reading of a Passion account, an extra Gospel on the Palm Sunday event, and pivotal readings from Isaiah 50 and Philippians 2, anyone would be at a loss to decide where to look, what to think, or how to feel. Since *less is almost always more when it comes to diving deep on the spiritual journey*, I hope you will be content with one meditation on one reading.

I am going to direct you toward the great parabolic movement described in the Second Reading of Philippians 2. Most consider that this was originally a hymn sung in the early Christian community, and certainly an inspired one on many levels. To give us an honest entrance-way into this profound text, let me offer you a life-changing quote from C.G. Jung's *Psychological Reflections:*

In the secret hour of life's midday the parabola is reversed, death is born. The second half of life does not signify ascent, unfolding, increase, exuberance, but death since the end is now its goal. The negation of life's fulfillment is synonymous with the refusal to accept its ending. Both mean not wanting to live, and not wanting to live is identical with not wanting to die. Waxing and waning make one curve.[1]

The hymn from Philippians artistically, honestly, but boldly describes that "secret hour" when God in Christ reversed the parabola, when the waxing became waning. It says it actually started with the great self-emptying or *kenosis* that we call the Incarnation in Bethlehem and ends with the Crucifixion in Jerusalem. It brilliantly connects the two mysteries as one movement, down, down, down into the enfleshment of creation, and then into humanity's depths and sadness, and final identification with those at the very bottom ("took the form of a slave") on the cross. Jesus represents God's total solidarity with, and even love of, the human situation, as if to say "nothing human is abhorrent to me." God, if Jesus is right, has chosen to descend—in almost total counterpoint with our humanity that is always trying to

NOTE

1. Jolande Jacobi, ed., *C.G. Jung, Psychological Reflections: A New Anthology of His Writings, 1905–1961* (Princeton, N.J.: Princeton University Press, 1970), p. 323.

climb, achieve, perform, and prove itself. He invites us to reverse the process too.

This hymn says that Jesus leaves the ascent to God, in God's way, and in God's time. What freedom! And it happens, better than any could have expected. "And because of this, God lifted him up, and gave him the name above all other names." We call it resurrection or ascension. Jesus is set as the human blueprint, the standard in the sky, the oh-so-hopeful pattern of divine transformation. Who would have presumed that the way up could be the way down? It is, as Paul says, "the Secret Mystery."

Trust the down, and God will take care of the up. This leaves humanity in solidarity with the life cycle, but also with one another, with no need to create success stories for itself, or to create failure stories for others. Humanity in Jesus is free to be human and soulful instead of any false climbing into "Spirit." This was supposed to change everything, and it still will.

Today's Reading

"Your mind must be the same as Christ's. Though he was in the form of God, he did not deem equality with God as something to be clung to. Instead he emptied himself, and became like a slave, and was born in the likeness of humanity...obediently accepting even death."

Philippians 2:5—7

Starter Prayer

"Lord Jesus, if you are indeed the Lord of History, then you are show-ing us the plan, direction, and meaning of the human journey. I want to speak like never before that 'Jesus Christ is Lord.' Now it is not an assertion of dominance or rightness over anybody else, but only a will-ingness to trust and follow your humble path."

MONDAY OF HOLY WEEK

The Servant of the "Servant of Yahweh"

Isaiah 42:1–7; John 12:1–11

I cannot find any obvious or clear connection between the two readings today. They both stand alone as masterpieces of revelation and of theology.

In Isaiah we have the first of the rightly named "Servant Songs," which will continue throughout the week. In these four accounts hidden away in Isaiah, one either sees a foretelling of Jesus in brilliant analysis, or one wonders if Jesus was "modeled" to fit these lovely descriptions. The correlation is uncanny, at any rate.

In the Gospel from John we have a woman acting as the "servant" to Jesus. (Maybe this is the connection?) We have Mary of Bethany again taking the fervent disciple's role instead of the hostess role of Martha. She anoints Jesus' feet with expensive nard, which is the anointing oil for death. My interpretation of this from all three varied Gospel accounts is that Mary is accepting the inevitability and necessity of death for Jesus (which Peter and the male inner circle cannot do!). "The whole house is filled with the fragrance."

Judas is the spokesman in the story, and he pretends to prefer the poor to a simple act of love. That is the clear point. It is forever a judgment on what we might now call "ideology on the left," a good balance after the text has heavily criticized the ideology of religious zealots and Pharisees on the "right." Jesus' response appears to be directly from Deuteronomy: "There will always be poor in the land. I command you therefore, always be open-handed with anyone in the country who is in need or is poor" (15:11).

Unfortunately, only the first phrase is quoted in the Gospel text, with the sad result that people have used this story to teach that religious piety is more important than social justice. As Paul will insightfully say later, "If I give away all that I possess, piece by piece, or even if I give away my body to be burned, but do not have love, it is useless" (1 Corinthians 13:3). As always, love of Jesus and love of justice for the neighbor are just two different shapes to the One Love.

Today's Reading

"He shall bring forth justice to the nations. But he will not cry out or make his voice heard in the street…until he establishes justice on the earth…. I, the Lord, have called you for the victory of justice…to open the eyes of the blind, and to bring out prisoners from confinement."

Isaiah 42:1—2, 4, 7

Starter Prayer

"God of love and justice, let me know and live that they are not separate. Loving people will do justice, and just people will do their work with love and respect."

TUESDAY OF HOLY WEEK
The Pain of Betrayal
Isaiah 49:1–6; John 13:21–33, 36–38

We continue on two powerful tracks, the second of the Servant Songs and the unfolding of the events leading up to Jesus' death in the Gospel. There is a poignant passage in the Servant Song that illustrates and prepares us for two betrayals that are about to happen: "I thought I had toiled in vain and uselessly, I have exhausted myself for nothing" (Isaiah 49:4). Surely that is the human feeling after someone we love turns against us. On some level, we all feel we have made some kind of contract with life, when life does not come through as we had hoped, and we feel a searing pain called betrayal. It happens to all of us in different ways. It is a belly punch that leaves us with a sense of futility and emptiness.

And here it happens to Jesus from two of his own inner circle, both Judas and Peter. The more love and hope you have invested in another person, the deeper the pain of betrayal is. If it happens at a deep and personal level, we wonder if he will ever trust again. Your heart does "break." It is one of those crossroad moments, when the breaking can forever close you down, or in time just the opposite—open you up to an enlargement of soul—as we will see in Jesus this week. What is happening is that we are withdrawing a human dependency, finding grace to forgive and let go, and relocating our little self in The Self (God), which never betrays us. It can't! It might take years for most of us to work through this; for Jesus it seems to have been natural, although who knows how long it took him to get there. All we see in the text is that there are no words of bitterness at all, only a calm, unblaming description in the midst of the "night," which is almost upon us.

Today's Reading

"'I tell you solemnly, one of you will betray me... Be quick about what you are to do' [Judas].... And it was night! ... 'you will lay down your life for me [Peter]? I tell you truly, the cock will not crow before you will have disowned me three times.'"

John 13:21, 27, 30, 38

Starter Prayer

"Solitary Jesus, you get more alone as the week goes on, till all you have is a naked but enduring hope in God. Do not bring me to such a test, I would not know how to survive."

WEDNESDAY OF HOLY WEEK
How Much Did Jesus Know and When Did He Know It?
Isaiah 50:4–9a; Matthew 26:14–25

Today we have the third Servant Song for our First Reading, which is a memorable set of striking images: "an open ear," "a well-trained tongue," that "knows how to speak to the weary." "I gave my back to those who beat me, my cheeks to those who plucked my beard, I did not shield my face from buffets and spitting…I have set my face like flint." (Isaiah 50:4–7). If this is ascribed to Jesus, as we Christians always have, then it clearly portrays one who is totally subject to the human condition, all the way to the bottom. He is a good listener and speaker, but in the end, his is an act of trust that another will "vindicate" him with utter confidence "that he will not be put to shame." The "Suffering Servant" here portrayed is a human being just like you and me. He does not know the outcome ahead of time, or his confidence would be in himself and God to pull it off, which would then largely be a matter of the willpower of belief. Faith is so much more than strong willpower

In Matthew's Gospel text, Jesus certainly appears to know ahead of time that Judas is going to betray him, and as much as tells him so. But he also appears to be saying that it is destiny or fate and "foretold by Scripture." Is this foreknowledge the pattern of the Suffering Servant that he is referring to? We do not know for sure, although John sees it predicted in Psalm 41:10: "Even my closest and most trusted friend, who shared my table, rebels against me," which he quotes (13:18). If this is the psalm Jesus is referring to, then the fuller meaning is clear: "Yahweh take pity on me, and raise me up!" (41:11). His victory is a dramatic reliance upon God, a mammoth leap of faith, not a superman stunt by a man who knows the full outcome ahead of time.

We have done the believing community a major disservice by so emphasizing his divinity that his humanity was all but overridden. "He did not really have to live faith or darkness as we do, he knew everything from his youngest years," most Christians naively assume. Yet Hebrews beautifully calls Jesus the "pioneer and perfector of our faith" (12:2). We cannot believe that his was a totally different brand of faith than the rest of humanity. Many scholars believe that it was only at the Resurrection that Jesus' human mind and divine consciousness became one. Until then, he "was like us in all ways, except sin" (Hebrews 4:15).

Now I believe you are much better prepared to walk through the sacred days ahead with a Jesus who shares, suffers, and trusts God exactly as you and I must learn to do. He walked in darkness too.

Today's Reading

"When it grew dark, he reclined at table with the Twelve. In the course of the meal he said, 'I tell you solemnly, one of you is about to betray me. Distressed at this, they began to say to him one after another, 'Surely it is not I, Lord?'"

Matthew 26:20–22

Starter Prayer

"Faithful Jesus, your faith was tried just like mine, but even more. Yet you trusted that you would not be put to shame, and 'into God's hands you entrusted your spirit.' Give me courage to do the same in the time of trial."

HOLY THURSDAY

Every Group Needs Its Ritual–Or the Message Is Lost and the Group Is Lost

Exodus 12:1–8, 11–14; John 13:1–15

As you would expect, we have three momentous readings for the day, and they are all in ritual settings. The older religions all understood the importance and power of group rituals. Without them, there is no memory, no re-creation of the founding myth for each new generation, no group cohesiveness, and no transformation of persons at the deeper levels of consciousness —and unconsciousness!

Because the message can be hardly missed in the Gospel, Jesus explicates it clearly, "As I have done, you also must do," and then in several more repetitions (John 13:13–20). But I am going to primarily talk about the First Reading from Exodus. Here Christians might be the most ignorant. The central Passover ritual defined this people: "This shall be a memorial feast for you, which all generations shall celebrate in Yahweh's honor as a perpetual institution" (Exodus 12:14).

I will only unpackage the central part of the ritual, but I think your Christian imagination will take it from there. Note that it says on the tenth day of the month ("April"), they are to procure a small year-old lamb for each household. They are to keep it for four days—just enough time for the children to bond with it and for all to see its loveliness—and then "slaughter it during the evening twilight"! Then they are to take its blood and sprinkle it on the doorpost of the houses. That night they are to eat it in highly ritualized fashion, recalling their departure from Egypt and their protection by God along the way. Thank God, the Jews eventually stopped animal sacrifice, but it was meant to be a psychic shock for all as killing always is. You can see, however, that the human psyche is slowly evolving in history to identify the real problem and what it is that actually has to die.

A cultural anthropologist could explain what is happening here. The sacrificial instinct is the deep recognition that something always has to die for something bigger to be born. We started with human sacrifice (Abraham and Isaac), we moved here to animal, and we gradually get closer to what really has to be sacrificed—our own beloved ego—as *protected and beloved as a little household lamb!* We will all find endless disguises and excuses to avoid letting go of what really needs to die for our own spiritual growth. And it is not other humans (firstborn sons of Egyptians), animals (lambs or goats), or even "meat on Friday" that God wants or needs. It is always our beloved passing self that has to be let go of. Jesus surely had a dozen good reasons why he should not have to die so young, so unsuccessful at that point, and the Son of God besides!

By becoming the symbolic Passover Lamb himself, plus the foot-washing servant in tonight's Gospel, *Jesus makes the movement to the human and the personal very clear and quite concrete.* It is always "we," in our youth, in our beauty, in our power and over-protectedness that must be handed over. Otherwise, we will never grow up, big enough to "eat" of the Mystery of God and Love. It really is about "passing over" to the next level of faith and life. And that never happens without some kind of "dying to the previous levels." This is an honest day of very good ritual that gathers all the absolutely essential but often avoided messages—necessary suffering, real sharing, divine intimacy, and loving servanthood.

Today's Readings

"This is how you are to eat it: with your loins girt, sandals on your feet and staff in hand, you shall eat like those who are going somewhere. This is the Passover of the Lord."

Exodus 12:11

"Jesus had loved his own in this world, and now wanted to show his love to them unto the end.... He took off his cloak, picked up a towel, poured water into a basin, and began to wash their feet."

John 13:1, 4–5

Starter Prayer

"On this holy night of prayer, I would like to 'spend one hour with you,' so you can teach me how I am to let go and how I am to live. Let me see your loveliness in bread and wine and song and even in the servant's towel."

GOOD FRIDAY

The Scapegoat and Scapegoating

Isaiah 52:13—53:12; John 18:1—19:42

Today the primary human problem, the core issue that defeats human history, is both revealed and resolved. It is indeed a "good" Friday. The central issue at work is the human inclination to kill others, in any multitude of ways, instead of dying ourselves—to our own illusions, pretenses, narcissism, and self-defeating behaviors. *Jesus dies "for" us not in the sense of "in place of" but "in solidarity with."* The first is merely a heavenly transaction of sorts; the second is a transformation of our very soul and the trajectory of history.

Cain has forever been killing Abel, the pattern is revealed from the very first children of Adam and Eve. Yet, thank God, and usually unnoticed, even Cain is "marked" for protection as he wanders East of Eden (Genesis 4:16). That marking became for Christians "the sign of the cross," our vaccination against killing—and being killed by our killing! But our vaccination did not always take; we who "worshiped" the Scapegoat usually became scapegoaters too. Always the problem was "elsewhere" than in ourselves, or merely outside instead of inside.

The soul needed one it could "gaze upon" long enough to know that it was *we who were doing the "piercing"* (John 19:37) *and we who were being pierced in doing it.* Jesus' body is a standing icon of what humanity is doing and what God suffers "with," "in," and "through" us. It is an icon of utter divine solidarity with our pain and our problems. It is both an external exposing and an eternal holding of the Great Mystery. It is our central transformative image for the soul. Whenever you see an image of the crucified Jesus, know that it is the clear and central message unveiled. It reveals what humanity is doing to itself and to one another. *Don't lessen its meaning by making it merely into a mechanical transaction whereby Jesus pays some "price" to God or the devil. The only price paid is to the intransigent human soul—so it can see!*

Humanity hates and attacks what it has every good reason to love— itself, God, and the rest of creation. It cannot say with Jesus, "Father, forgive them all, they do not know what they are doing" (Luke 23:34). None of us really knows what we are doing until the outer crucifix becomes the inner revelation of every act of human barbarism, war, torture, starvation, disease, abuse, oppression, injustice, early death, and absurd lives "from the blood of Abel the Holy to the blood of Zechariah whom you killed" (Matthew 23:35)! These are the first and last murders in the Jewish Bible of Jesus' time, and Jesus seems to see them as one collective. It is the same and consistent human blindness since the beginning of time.

On the cross, the veil between the Holy and the unholy is "torn from top to bottom" (Matthew 27:51), the "curtain of his body" becomes a "living opening" (Hebrews 10:20) through which we all can now walk into the Holy of Holies, which on different levels is both our own soul and the very heart of God. *Nothing changed in heaven on Good Friday, but everything potentially changed on earth.* Some learned how to see and to trust the contract between God and humanity. God has always and forever loved what God created, "It was good, it was very good" (Genesis 1:31). It was we who could not love and see the omnipresent goodness. We were trapped outside the veil.

But now, as our Second Reading says today, we can "confidently approach the throne of grace to receive mercy and favor" (Hebrews 4:16). The curtain is, and always has been, wide open, as we see dramatized in the naked body and bleeding heart of Jesus, which we Catholics call "the Sacred Heart." It seems we needed an image that shocking, dramatic, and compelling or we just could not get the point, see ourselves, or trust the Great Love.

Today's Readings

"Yet it was our infirmities that he bore, our sufferings that he endured… He was pierced for our offenses, and crushed for our sins, upon him was the chastisement that makes us whole." [Now do not think of this as an act of suffering for nearly as much as an act of suffering with. It makes a major difference.]

Isaiah 53:4—5

"'Now it is finished.' [The lie is over.] And he bowed his head and gave up His Spirit.'" [The truth was handed on to history.]

John 19:30

Starter Prayer

"Crucified Jesus, you are not a stranger to my soul, you are not foreign to our history. You have revealed, resolved, and forgiven it all on the cross. I join the whole world today in thanking you. This is indeed a good Friday."

HOLY SATURDAY
Liminal Space
Luke 24:1–12

"After a day or two Yahweh will bring us back to life; on the third day God will raise us up, and we shall live in his presence." (Hosea 6:2)

Limen is the Latin word for threshold. A "liminal space" is the crucial in-between time—when everything actually happens and yet nothing appears to be happening. It is the waiting period when the cake bakes, the movement is made, the transformation takes place. One cannot just jump from Friday to Sunday in this case, there must be Saturday! This, of course, was always the holyday for the Jewish tradition. The Sabbath rest was the pivotal day for the Jews, and even the dead body of Jesus rests on Saturday, waiting for God to do whatever God plans to do. It is our great act of trust and surrender, both together. A new "creation *ex nihilo*" is about to happen, but first it must be desired.

For all of us this is the necessary "handing over time," when soul and Spirit rejoin with body. Now we call it necessary "grief work." Time is in connivance with Eternity and Eternity does not play outside of its rules. The first mystery must be contained, suffered, and contemplated before the new birth can take place. The tomb is temporarily a womb.

"They laid the body in a tomb that had been cut into the rock, and rolled a stone across the entrance," says Mark's Gospel. Luke has the women "watch," and then they go home to prepare spices and perfumes, and "observe the Sabbath as a day of rest." Greatness does not just happen unprepared. It must be waited for, needed, desired, and an inner space must be created. The Sabbath rest is everything—and yet nothing. Just like the soul and like the Spirit.

Tonight the church will celebrate its central liturgy for the entire church year. All pivots around this night and this necessary transformation of the soul. Yes, Jesus is the one who walks it consciously first, but it is so that we can trustfully follow. Tomorrow *will* be different than today. One must have walked through this Mystery at least once—on some level of real life—or it is just pretty ritual and rarefied belief. Augustine rightly named it the "paschal mystery" or the mystery of passing over.

I will end with that, so you can entrust yourself now to a life passage that is beyond any of my words to get you there, or any proof that it really happened for Jesus. You finally have to walk it yourself. When the whole cycle happens to you, you will know it could well have happened to Jesus, and maybe even did! Now you are ready for Sunday, the first day of the week, the ever-new day of Resurrected Life, which will allow you henceforth to read all your life backward and understand, and read it forward with hope.

Remember, hope is not some vague belief that "all will work out well," but *biblical hope is the certainty that things finally have a victorious meaning no matter how they turn out.* We learned that from Jesus, which gives us now the courage to live our lives forward from here. Maybe that is the full purpose of Lent.

Today's Reading

"On the first day of the week, at first light, the women came to the tomb bringing the spices they had prepared. They found the stone rolled back from the tomb, but when they entered, they did not find the body of the Lord Jesus."

Luke 24:1–2

Starter Prayer

"Ever Risen Christ, you have taken me into your mystery of passion, death, waiting, and new life. Because I trust you, I trust my own dyings too. Allow me this Easter to go all the way with you, and to now trust our Eternal Sunday even more than any Passing Friday or Waiting Saturday. Amen."

ABOUT THE AUTHOR

Franciscan priest RICHARD ROHR is founder and animator of the Center for Action and Contemplation in Albuquerque, New Mexico. Author of numerous books, including *Hope Against Darkness: The Transforming Vision of Saint Francis in an Age of Anxiety* with John Feister and *Things Hidden: Scripture as Spirituality*, he gives retreats and lectures internationally.